creative ideas
for kids' rooms

Sieta Lambrias

creative ideas
for kids' rooms

**Great ideas for children of all ages,
over 25 step-by-step projects**

hamlyn

First published in Great Britain in 2007 by Hamlyn,
a division of Octopus Publishing Group Ltd
2–4 Heron Quays, London E14 4JP

ISBN-13: 978-0-600-61495-1
ISBN-10: 0-600-61495-6

A CIP catalogue record for this book is available
from the British Library

Printed and bound in China

10 9 8 7 6 5 4 3 2 1

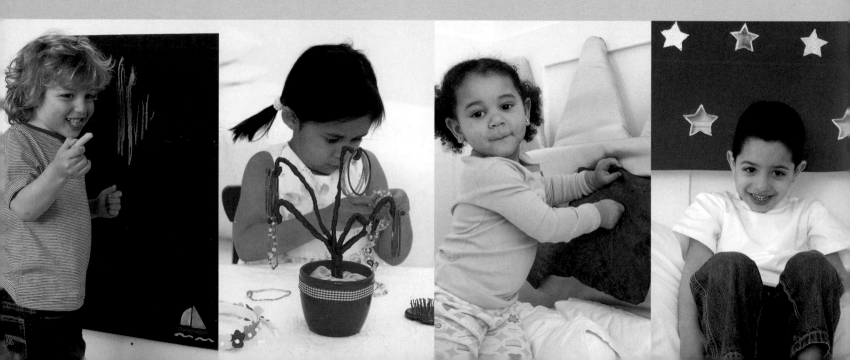

contents

introduction

A child's room is not just for sleeping in, but is a very personal space in which he or she can play, learn and entertain friends. Although they may vary in size, successful children's bedrooms always fulfil a number of key requirements.

Naturally, a bed is a must, but there are other things to consider. Would your child benefit from having a desk? Is there adequate storage for toys, art materials and books? Could there be a better selection of soft furnishings? Is the room decorated to suit your child's tastes and age? Above all, is it a room in which your child enjoys spending time?

There are countless ways that you can make your child's room a very special and fun place to be, and you will find a good number of them here. This book offers over 25 projects that include ideas for innovative storage and lighting, for adapting furniture to suit both work and play and for creating rooms with a specific theme.

Calling on basic DIY, needlework and craft skills, the projects are easy to complete – mostly within a day – and they can all be adapted to suit designs and schemes of your own making.

Your children can even join in, helping to put the finishing touches to a project and making his or her own personal contribution.

Outfitting a child's room can be a costly business, particularly as their tastes change dramatically with age and the latest fashions. For this reason, the projects in this book focus on accessorizing a room rather than re-decorating it completely. Ideas include those for revamping existing furniture and bedding, as well as for producing multifunctional furniture or toys in order to maximize on space and minimize on expense.

The real advantage of this book is that the projects can be adapted simply by changing the theme, or by adding new and different elements. So, although there are over 25 projects to work from initially, with a little creative thought, the number of ways in which you can change your child's room is far greater.

work and play

drop-leaf flower desk

This pretty little desk provides an ideal focal point for a pink floral room. Have fun with your daughter in creating a design of your own, keeping the overall shape simple but using your imagination for the colour scheme and painted detail.

 intermediate

 6 hours (including drying time)

 girls

 suitable for a helping hand

you will need

- Planed pine:
  75 x 50 cm x 18 mm
  (30 x 20 x ¾ in) for the top
  35 x 35 cm x 18 mm
  (14 x 14 x ¾ in) for the support
  25 x 5 cm (10 x 2 in) for piece B
  7.5 x 7.5 cm (3 x 3 in) for piece D
  75 x 7.5 cm x 18 mm
  (30 x 3 x ¾ in) for piece A
  75 x 6 cm x 18 mm
  (30 x 2¼ x ¾ in) for piece C
- Pencil
- Eraser
- Jigsaw
- Dust mask
- Circular saw
- Sanding block
- Fine-grade sandpaper
- 250 ml (8 fl oz) wood primer
- 2.5 cm (1 in) paintbrush
- Tape measure
- Five 4 cm (1½ in) butt hinges with screws
- Screwdriver
- Satinwood paint:
  250 ml (8 fl oz) pink
  250 ml (8 fl oz) beige
  250 ml (8 fl oz) green
- Acrylic paint:
  125 ml (4 fl oz) fuchsia pink
  125 ml (4 fl oz) gold
- Fine artist's paintbrush
- Router
- Two 12 mm (½ in) screws
- Drill and drill bits
- PVA glue
- Two 4 cm (1½ in) 'L'-shaped brackets with screws
- Spirit level
- Six Rawlplugs
- Six 2.5 cm (1 in) screws

1 Using the illustration as a guide (see right), draw one half of a flower shape, freehand, on the pine desk top in pencil, erasing any lines you are unhappy with. Cut out the shape using a jigsaw.

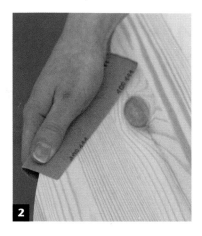

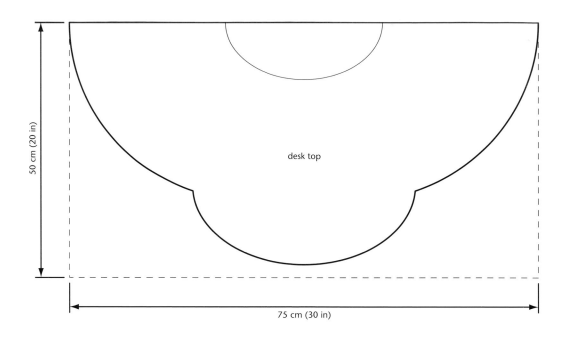

50 cm (20 in)

desk top

75 cm (30 in)

2 Cut the wood for the support in half diagonally using a circular saw. Saw off the sharp tips of the two non-right-angle corners of one triangle. Cut pieces B and D from the remaining triangle (see page 10 for measurements). Sand all edges smooth, then prime all surfaces using the 2.5 cm (1 in) paintbrush and leave to dry.

3 Follow the diagram (see opposite) to assemble the desk. Abut one long edge of piece A to the straight edge of the flower-shaped top. Measure and mark 35 cm (14 in) in from one end and secure one hinge here, making sure that both pieces of wood are flush. Attach 2 more hinges 2.5 cm (1 in) in from each end in the same way.

4 Turn the whole assembly over and follow the photograph opposite to draw flower details over the desk and the attached length of wood.

Paint the top of the desk in pink and beige using the 2.5 cm (1 in) paintbrush and, when dry, add finer details in fuchsia pink and gold using the artist's paintbrush. Leave to dry completely before folding the hinged section down and painting the edges to match. Paint the triangular support green.

5 Rout out a section down the centre of piece B, 2 cm (⅞ in) wide x 6 mm (¼ in) deep. Use two 12 mm (½ in) screws to secure this piece of wood to the centre of the underside of the flower.

6 Attach two hinges to the bottom edge of the right-angled painted support (see diagram), one 32 cm (12½ in) down from the corner, and one 2.5 cm (1 in) in from the corner. Centre piece D on the top hinge of the support and attach. Drill two holes either side of the hinge for fixing to the wall.

7 Drill four holes along the length of piece C: two at 2.5 cm (1 in) in from each end and two at 20 cm (8 in) in from each end. Run some PVA glue along one long 18 mm (¾ in) edge of piece C and abut to piece A as shown.

8 Measure 15 cm (6 in) from each end of piece C and attach the two 'L'-shaped brackets in order to secure the join between pieces A and C.

9 To attach the desk to your wall hold it in position while you mark the drilling holes on the wall. Be sure to use a spirit level. Remove the desk, drill the holes and insert a Rawlplug in each before screwing the desk to the wall with 2.5 cm (1 in) screws. Lift the desk top and insert the support into the routed groove on piece B to secure the top when in use.

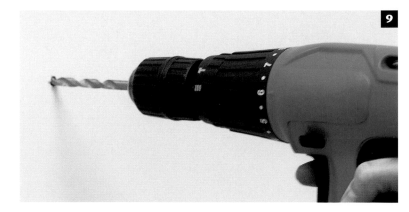

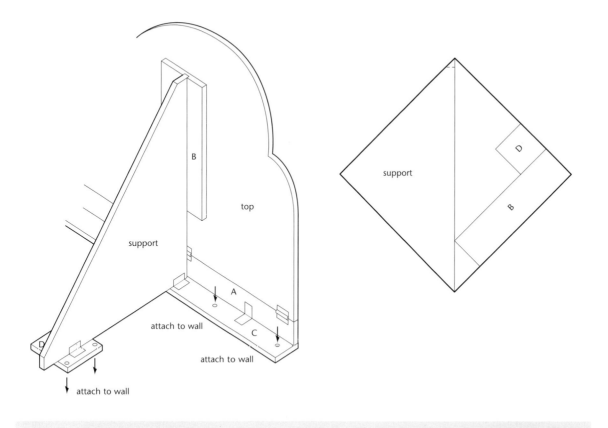

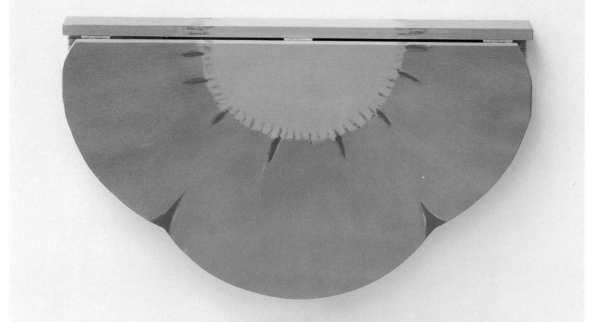

 Top tips

• Using a soft wood will make it easier to screw on the fixings.

• Paint piece C the same colour as the bedroom wall so that it blends into the background, making the desk alone stand out.

★ **Try this**

Have fun drawing and painting the corresponding half of the flower on the wall to complete the shape.

Create a flower notice board to match the desk by sticking cork tiles to the wall above the desk and painting them to match the flower.

See also...

• Pretty Pocket Bed Throw, on page 52.

• Butterfly Handles, on page 112.

three-way chalkboard

A great multipurpose activity centre, this project combines a chalkboard, a corkboard and a magnetic notice board with a pencil box, offering your child great scope for creativity. The simple design allows the board to be stored flat against the wall when not in use.

 intermediate

 5 hours (including drying time)

 girls and boys

 suitable for a helping hand

you will need

- Planed pine:
  75 x 50 cm x 18 mm
    (30 x 20 x ¾ in) for piece A
  75 x 7.5 cm x 18 mm
    (30 x 3 in x ¾ in) for piece B
  75 x 6 cm x 18 mm
    (30 x 2¼ x ¾ in) for piece C
- 250 ml (8 fl oz) wood primer
- 2.5 cm (1 in) paintbrush
- Paint:
  125 ml (4 fl oz) blackboard paint
  125 ml (4 fl oz) sky blue matt emulsion paint
  Small tube yellow acrylic paint
  Small tube red acrylic paint
- Wooden pencil box:
  20 x 5 x 2.5 cm (8 x 2 x 1 in)
- 12.5 x 12.5 cm (5 x 5 in) acetate for stencil (see Templates, page 132)
- Fine black felt-tip pen
- Craft knife

- Cutting mat
- Ruler
- Masking tape
- Fine artist's paintbrush
- Tape measure
- Pencil
- Three 4 cm (1½ in) butt hinges with screws
- Screwdriver
- PVA glue
- 58.5 x 38 cm (23 x 15 in) white magnetic notice board
- Drill and drill bits
- Two 4 cm (1½ in) 'L'-shaped brackets with screws
- Spirit level
- Four Rawlplugs
- Four 2.5 cm (1 in) screws
- 58.5 x 38 cm (23 x 15 in) corkboard
- Eight 12 mm (½ in) double-sided adhesive foam pads

1 Prime all three pieces of pine using the 2.5 cm (1 in) paintbrush and leave to dry. Paint one side and all edges of piece A and the pencil box using blackboard paint. When dry, paint the other side of piece A sky blue, along with pieces B and C.

2 Use the boat template on page 133 to make an acetate stencil. Position the stencil at the bottom right-hand corner of the blackboard using masking tape to secure it in place. Paint the boat yellow, red and blue using the fine artist's paintbrush. Once dry, paint in the waves below the boat freehand.

3 Follow the diagram (see left) to assemble the three-way chalkboard. Take piece A and place it flat on the floor, blue side up. Abut the long edge of piece B to one long edge of piece A and join the two using the butt hinges. Position the first hinge in the centre – 35 cm (14 in) in from one edge – and the other two 2.5 cm (1 in) in from each edge.

4 Use PVA glue to attach the magnetic notice board and pencil box, the right way up, in the centre of the blue panel.

5 Now drill four holes along the length of piece C: two at 2.5 cm (1 in) from each end and two at 20 cm (8 in) in from either end. Run some PVA glue along one long 18 mm (¾ in) edge of piece C and attach to piece B as shown.

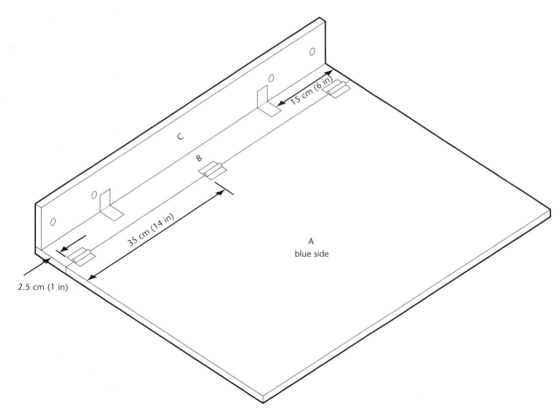

15 cm (6 in)

C

B

35 cm (14 in)

A
blue side

2.5 cm (1 in)

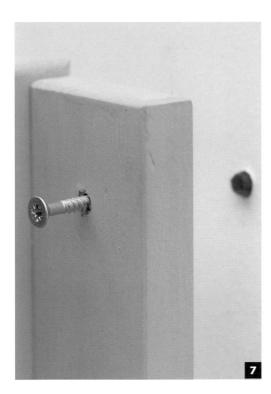

6 Measure 15 cm (6 in) in from each end of piece C and attach the two 'L' shaped brackets in order to secure the join between pieces B and C.

7 To attach the chalkboard to your wall hold it in position while you mark the drilling positions on the wall. Be sure to use a spirit level. Remove the chalkboard, drill the holes and insert a Rawlplug in each before screwing the chalkboard to the wall.

8 Complete the project by attaching a corkboard to the wall behind the chalkboard using double-sided adhesive foam pads. Simply position them on the back of the board, at equal distances around the edge.

 Top tip

• Paint the reverse side of the chalkboard in a satinwood or soft-sheen paint for a wipe-clean finish.

★ Try this

Stencil a boat onto the cork notice board to continue the nautical theme.

See also...

• Treasure-chest Table, on page 30.

football
notice board

Complete a football-themed room by transforming a plain cork notice board into the perfect pitch display board. Not only will it encourage your child to keep drawings, cards and souvenirs as a tidy display, he can also have fun helping you to make it.

easy

1 hour
(not including
drying time)

boys

suitable for a
helping hand

you will need

- 60 x 40 cm (24 x 16 in) cork
  notice board
- Matt emulsion or poster paint:
  125 ml (4 fl oz) green
  125 ml (4 fl oz) white
  small tube blue
  small tube red
- 2.5 cm (1 in) paintbrush
- Medium artist's paintbrush
- 12 wooden clothes pegs
- Black felt-tip pen
- Pencil
- Ruler
- 12.5 cm (5 in) diameter small bowl
  or cup
- PVA glue

1 Paint the cork area of the board using the green paint and the 2.5 cm (1 in) paintbrush. Use the artist's brush to paint the wooden frame white. Leave to dry.

2 Taking each clothes peg in turn, use the black felt-tip pen to draw a thin line across the bottom to represent the player's boots. Use the artist's brush to paint the shorts white, from the grooved section to about halfway down (the other half is left 'natural' for the legs). Paint the top section blue or red for the 'shirt' colours – you need six pegs of each colour.

3 Once the cork notice board is dry, mark out the lines for a simple football pitch with a pencil and a ruler. Use a small bowl to draw the circle and semi-circles. Paint over your lines in white, using the artist's brush. You could paint against the ruler and bowl for a neater finish, but wash any paint off them immediately afterwards.

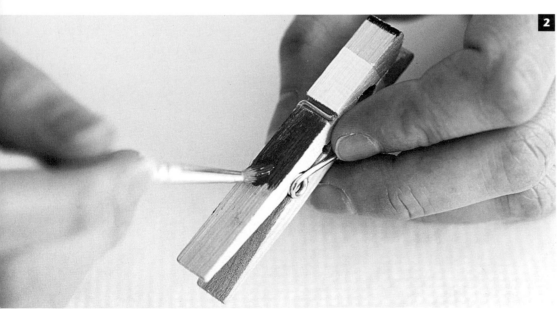

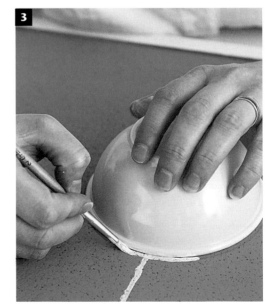

4 When all the paint is dry, position the painted pegs on the pitch. When happy with the arrangement, glue each one to the board.

5 Once the glue is dry, the board can be used for pegging up tickets, photos, match mementoes, league tables – anything your child fancies.

① Top tips

• Add players' numbers to the shirts using the black felt-tip pen. Remember to let the paint dry first!

• If you want to move the pegs around, attach a piece of thick green felt within the frame instead of painting the surface. By sticking the hook half of hook-and-loop fastener to the back of the pegs, you can attach and detach them from the board at will.

★ Try this

Paint the cork area midnight blue for a cosmic theme. Cut out card stars or circles for planets and paint appropriately. Stick them onto the pegs before gluing the pegs to the board.

See also...

• Goal! Bed, on page 44.

noughts and crosses cushion

This is a novel idea for a floor cushion, where the cover provides children with a noughts and crosses board using felt pieces, as well as somewhere comfortable to lounge! The idea is so simple that it can be adapted easily for any room scheme.

 intermediate

 5 hours

 girls and boys

 suitable for a helping hand

you will need

- Fabric:
  180 x 90 cm (72 x 36 in) blue denim
  95 x 30 cm (74 x 12 in) cream cotton
  60 x 60 cm (24 x 24 in) red felt
- Scissors
- Tape measure
- Iron and board
- Dressmaking chalk
- Ruler
- Sewing pins
- Sewing machine

- Sewing thread:
  Cream
  Blue
- 90 cm x 12 mm (36 x ½ in) sew-on hook-and-loop fastener
- Two 20 x 20 cm (8 x 8 in) squares of card for templates (see Templates, page 132)
- Glue
- Fine black felt-tip pen
- 85 x 85 cm (35½ x 35½ in) cushion pad

1 Fold the blue denim fabric in half lengthways and cut to make two 90 x 90 cm (36 x 36 in) squares. Cut the cream cotton fabric into four equal lengths measuring 95 x 7.5 cm (74 x 3 in). Fold each of the cream lengths in by 12 mm (½ in) along the long edge and iron the folds flat, to give you four 5 cm (2 in) wide cream strips.

2 Lay one denim panel out flat, right side up, and use dressmaking chalk and a ruler to mark a noughts and crosses grid, with vertical lines and horizontal lines at 30 cm (12 in) intervals.

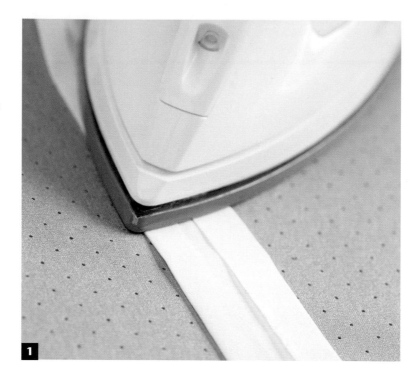

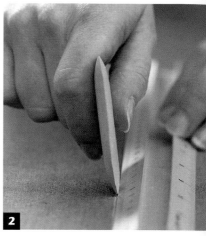

3 Centre one cream strip over each of the vertical chalk grid lines and pin in place. Repeat with the horizontal grid lines. Once happy with the layout, machine-stitch into place with the cream thread.

4 Lay the second denim panel over the first, right sides together, making sure both panels are lying flat and square. Pin a 2.5 cm (1 in) hem on three sides and machine-stitch with blue thread.

5 Pin the 'hook' half of the fabric fastener along one unstitched side of the cushion cover, and the 'loop' half along the opposite edge. Machine-stitch in place. Turn the cushion cover right way out, and insert the cushion pad, closing the hook-and-loop fastener.

6 To complete the project, make card templates of the noughts and crosses on page 133. Use a fine felt-tip pen to mark five of each on the red felt and cut out using scissors.

6

 Top tips

• This project can be made in any size: simply measure your own cushion and adapt the measurements to suit.

• Stitch or appliqué a pocket to the back of the cushion to keep the pieces safe when not in play.

★ **Try this**

Adapt the project to suit any room by choosing different-coloured fabrics or by making felt flowers and butterflies for a garden theme, for example.

See also...

• Domino Toy Boxes, on page 82.

• CD Screen, on page 78.

jigsaw wall art

This is a quick-and-easy project for introducing colour to a child's room. Encourage your child to help you by choosing the jigsaw colours for each letter, and use the finished board to help to teach the alphabet or to start making first words.

easy

2 hours

girls and boys

suitable for a
helping hand

you will need

- 7.5 x 7.5 cm (3 x 3 in) card for template (see Templates, page 132)
- Glue
- Craft scissors
- Fine felt-tip pen
- Foam sheets:
  30 x 21 cm (12 x 8¼ in) pink
  30 x 21 cm (12 x 8¼ in) blue
  30 x 21 cm (12 x 8¼ in) green
  30 x 21 cm (12 x 8¼ in) yellow

- Self-adhesive foam letters alphabet, each 2.5 cm (1 in)
- 32.5 x 1.25 cm (10 x ½ in) self-adhesive magnetic strip
- 60 x 40 cm (24 x 16 in) magnetic notice board
- 125 ml (4 fl oz) green matt emulsion paint
- 1.25 cm (½ in) paintbrush
- Eight 12 mm (½ in) double-sided adhesive foam pads

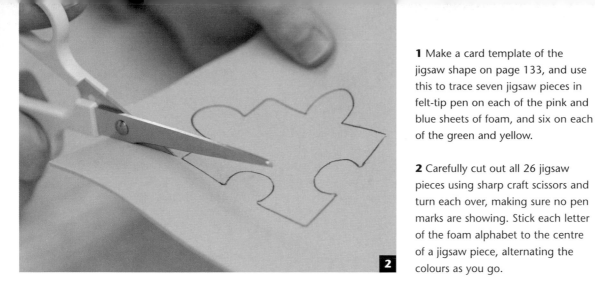

1 Make a card template of the jigsaw shape on page 133, and use this to trace seven jigsaw pieces in felt-tip pen on each of the pink and blue sheets of foam, and six on each of the green and yellow.

2 Carefully cut out all 26 jigsaw pieces using sharp craft scissors and turn each over, making sure no pen marks are showing. Stick each letter of the foam alphabet to the centre of a jigsaw piece, alternating the colours as you go.

 Top tip

• The design of the jigsaw template means that pieces can be arranged to either side, above and below each other, keeping the project simple but very versatile.

3 Cut the magnetic strip into 26 equal-sized pieces (approximately 12 mm/½ in long), and stick each length onto the back of a foam jigsaw piece.

★ **Try this**

Use the same principle to turn a family portrait or a photograph of your child into a jigsaw work of art. Simply stick the photo to a sheet of foam and cut out using the jigsaw template once dry.

See also...

• Jigsaw Cushions, on page 56.

4 Paint the wooden frame of the magnetic board in green and leave to dry. You can attach the board to the wall using the foam pads. Simply position them on the back of the board, at equal distances around the edge.

treasure-chest table

Revamp an old toy box to make this treasure-chest table. Not only will it make a fun surface to work at, but it will also provide plenty of storage for a host of drawing and painting materials. Your child will have fun helping you with the painting and sponging.

 intermediate

 4 hours

 girls and boys

 suitable for a helping hand

you will need

- Wooden toy box, approximately 79 x 48 x 43 cm (31 x 19 x 17 in)
- Screwdriver
- 100 x 80 cm x 18 mm (40 x 36 x ¾ in) sheet of medium-density fibreboard (MDF)
- Tape measure
- Pencil
- Jigsaw
- Dust mask
- Sanding block
- Fine-grade sandpaper
- 500 ml (17 fl oz) wood primer
- Paint tray
- Small paint roller
- 2.5 cm (1 in) paintbrush
- Satinwood paint:
  500 ml (1 pt) light blue
  125 ml (4 fl oz) royal blue
  125 ml (4 fl oz) red
  125 ml (4 fl oz) green
  125 ml (4 fl oz) yellow
  125 ml (4 fl oz) white

- 40 x 30 cm (16 x 12 in) acetate for stencils (see Templates, page 132)
- Fine black felt-tip pen
- Craft knife
- Cutting mat
- Ruler
- Masking tape
- Fine artist's paintbrush
- 15 x 7.5 x 2.5 cm (6 x 3 x 1 in) sponge
- Scissors
- Two small plates

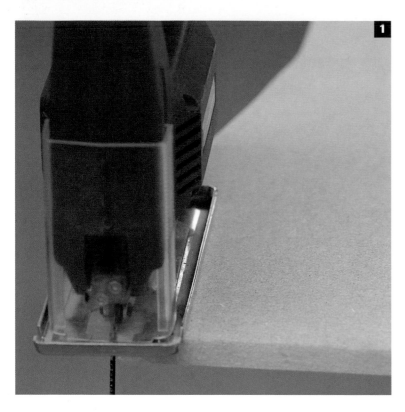

1 Remove the existing lid of the toy box, keeping the hinges and screws. Cut the MDF panel to the same length as the old lid. For the depth, you need to add at least a 20 cm (8 in) overhang to allow for legroom. Draw a wavy edge along the front of the lid and cut out using a jigsaw.

2 Sand all surfaces smooth. Prime both the new lid and toy box using the small roller and, once dry, fit the new lid to the toy chest using the original screws and hinges. Paint the assembled toy chest light blue.

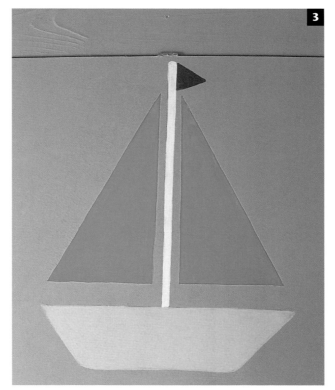

3 Make acetate stencils of the boat and anchor using the templates on page 134, and varying the size depending on your design. Position a large boat stencil in the centre of the lid and, if necessary, secure with masking tape to keep it in place. Paint the boat in green, yellow, white and red using the fine artist's paintbrush. Continue to decorate the toy box in the same way, using smaller boat stencils, and position the yellow anchor on the front of the box.

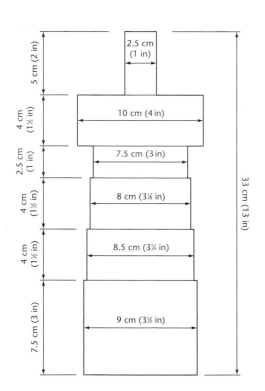

5 cm (2 in)

2.5 cm (1 in)

4 cm (1½ in)

10 cm (4 in)

2.5 cm (1 in)

7.5 cm (3 in)

4 cm (1½ in)

8 cm (3⅛ in)

4 cm (1½ in)

8.5 cm (3¼ in)

33 cm (13 in)

7.5 cm (3 in)

9 cm (3½ in)

4 Follow the measurements given on the illustration (opposite) to cut six rectangular shapes from the large sponge using scissors. Pour some red and white paint onto separate plates and use the sponges in sequence, starting at the bottom, to create the lighthouse on each end of the box, red first, then white, and so on. Complete the effect by painting, freehand, the red dome at the top of the lighthouse (see illustration for approximate height), and the yellow beaming light, using the fine artist's paintbrush.

5 To finish the chest, draw a simple wave pattern in pencil around the sides of the chest and along the front edge of the lid and paint in royal blue.

 Top tips

• Make sure that the thickness of the MDF is the same as that of the lid you are replacing.

• Keep the shape of the lid as basic as possible to allow for comfort while sitting at the desk.

• Use satinwood or eggshell paint for easy-wipe surfaces or finish with a coat of clear satinwood varnish.

★ Try this

Any theme can be painted onto the chest: simply take your lead from your child's existing room scheme.

See also...

• Three-way Chalkboard, on page 14.

rest and relax

rainbow curtain

This colourful curtain has been made to fit a 90 cm (36 in) wide window, but its simple construction means that you can easily adapt the measurements of both the pelmet and curtain to fit any window width. The method assumes you already have a curtain rail in place.

intermediate

6 hours

girls and boys

not suitable for a helping hand

you will need

- Fabric:
  200 x 140 cm (80 x 56 in)
    orange cotton
  200 x 140 cm (80 x 56 in)
    yellow cotton
  200 x 140 cm (80 x 56 in)
    green cotton
  200 x 140 cm (80 x 56 in)
    blue cotton
  200 x 140 cm (80 x 56 in)
    purple cotton
  200 x 140 cm (80 x 56 in)
    red cotton
  40 x 40 cm (16 x 16 in)
    buckram for star
  100 x 50 cm (40 x 20 in)
    buckram for pelmet
  100 x 140 cm (40 x 56 in)
    interlining
- Tape measure
- Sharp scissors
- Pencil

- 12 mm (½ in) paintbrush
- Iron and board
- 170 x 15 cm (68 x 6 in)
    bonding web
- Fabric glue
- Needle
- Tacking thread
- Sewing machine
- Sewing thread:
  Purple
  Blue
  Green
  Orange
  Red
- 200 x 2.5 cm (80 x 1 in)
    curtain tape
- 90 x 5 x 5 cm (36 x 2 x 2 in)
    pine baton
- Drill and drill bits
- Spirit level
- Two 7.5 cm (3 in) screws
- Two Rawlplugs

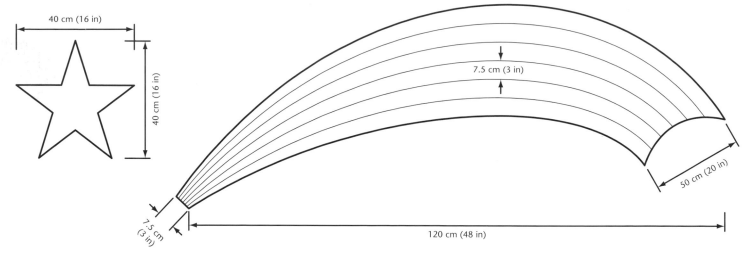

40 cm (16 in)

40 cm (16 in)

7.5 cm (3 in)

50 cm (20 in)

7.5 cm (3 in)

120 cm (48 in)

3 Centre the buckram star on the interlining, wet the edges with a paintbrush and fold the excess fabric over. Press firmly with an iron to fix. Repeat to cover the buckram pelmet with interlining.

4 Cut a star from yellow fabric, making it 10 mm (⅜ in) bigger all round. Centre the buckram star, interlining side down, on the yellow star (wrong side up) and attach as above.

5 Follow the illustration (see above) to cut the rainbow strips for the pelmet to a length of 120 x 7.5 cm (48 x 3 in) each (cut down as required to follow your template), starting with purple, and adding 10 mm (⅜ in) at each short end for fixing to the back of the buckram. Use bonding web and an iron to fix the purple strip to the bottom of the buckram rainbow before wetting the back of the buckram to fix the short edges.

1 Start by preparing the fabric strips for the curtain. Measure and cut a 200 x 33 cm (80 x 13 in) strip from each of the orange, yellow, green and blue fabrics. From each of the purple and red fabrics, cut a 200 x 35.5 cm (80 x 14 in) strip.

2 Using the illustration as a guide (see above), draw the star and rainbow shapes, either freehand onto the buckram or enlarging onto a grid to make a template. Cut out the buckram star and rainbow using sharp scissors. Cut the interlining fabric for the buckram star, making it 5 mm (⅛ in) bigger all round.

38 rest and relax

6 For the subsequent strips, iron flat a 10 mm (⅜ in) hem along the bottom of the strip before attaching with bonding web so that it overlaps the previous strip by 5 mm (⅛ in). Once you have bonded all of the strips in place, turn the buckram over, wet the edges and firmly press and fix all fabric ends into place.

7 To complete the pelmet, use strong fabric glue to attach the fabric star to the pointed end of the rainbow and leave to dry.

8 Stitch the pre-cut fabric curtain strips together in rainbow order, starting with purple and using a French seam: first lay two adjoining strips wrong sides together. Tack and machine-stitch along one long edge, taking a 5 mm (⅛ in) seam. Turn the fabrics strips right sides together and iron. Now tack and machine-stitch the same long edge, taking a 10 mm (⅜ in) seam to enclose the raw edges.

9 Along the outer edges, make a 2 cm (¾ in) double turning and stitch close to the edge. Stitch a double hem 7.5 cm (3 in) at the bottom. Fold over the top edge by 2.5 cm (1 in) and stitch on the curtain tape.

10 Mount the pelmet before hanging the curtain. Measure, mark and drill two holes in the pine baton 20 cm (8 in) in from each end. Centre the baton above the window to mark the drilling positions, using a spirit level. Drill the holes and insert a Rawlplug before screwing the baton in place.

11 Run PVA glue along the baton and secure the rainbow pelmet in place. Hang the curtain.

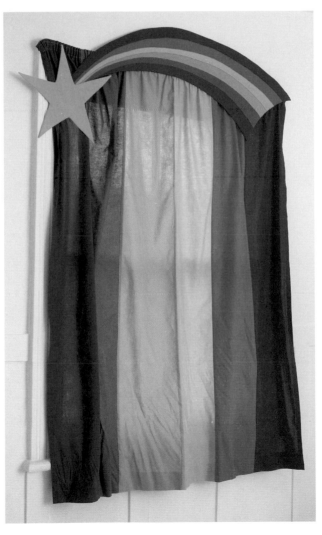

(!) Top tips

• When attaching the pelmet to the pine baton, check its position carefully to make sure it fully conceals the curtain rail and hooks.

• When sewing the rainbow curtain strips together, always use a sewing thread that matches the colour of the darker fabric.

★ Try this

Make a matching roller blind. Cut equal-width strips of the rainbow fabrics with a suitable drop for your window. Machine-stitch using French seams and attach to a do-it-yourself roller-blind mechanism.

See also...

• Pot of Gold Nightlight, on page 86.

fire-engine bed

This fire-engine curtain pane will bring a dramatic new look to your son's bed. Suitable for a raised or bunk bed, it is easy to attach once completed and will provide hours of play for budding little fire fighters.

 intermediate

 6 hours

 boys

 not suitable for a helping hand

you will need

- Fabric:
  150 x 150 cm (60 x 60 in)
    red cotton
  178 x 38 cm (70 x 15 in)
    yellow cotton
  20 x 20 cm (8 x 8 in)
    blue cotton
  50 x 50 cm (20 x 20 in)
    silver poly cotton
  50 x 50 cm (20 x 20 in)
    black cotton
- Tape measure
- Scissors
- Sewing pins
- Sewing machine

- Sewing thread:
  Red
  Yellow
  Black
  Blue
- 40 x 30 cm (16 x 12 in) paper for template (see Templates, page 132)
- Compass
- Pencil
- 15 x 15 x 2.5 cm (6 x 6 x 1 in) wadding
- Yellow embroidery thread
- 400 cm x 12 mm (160 x ½ in) self-adhesive hook-and-loop fastener

1 Prepare the fabrics. From the red fabric, measure and cut a 105 x 145 cm (42 x 58 in) panel. Pin a 2.5 cm (1 in) hem around the four sides and machine-stitch using red thread. From the yellow fabric, measure and cut a 17.5 x 142.5 cm (7 x 57 in) panel. Pin a 2.5 cm (1 in) hem around the four sides and machine-stitch using yellow thread.

2 To make the windows, cut two rectangles from the silver fabric, one 45 x 12.5 cm (18 x 5 in) and one 35 x 32.5 cm (14 x 13 in). Pin a 12 mm (½ in) hem all around and machine-stitch to secure, using black thread. On the thinner rectangle, turn a corner under by 2.5 cm (1 in) to give a curved edge.

3 To make the window frames, cut the following 2.5 cm (1 in) wide strips of black fabric. For window 1: 45 cm (18 in) for the long straight edge; 20 cm (8 in) for top and bottom edges (to allow for curved window front); and 35.5 cm (14 in) for the shorter straight edge. For window 2: two 35 cm (14 in) strips and two 32.5 cm (13 in) strips. Fold each strip in half lengthways, pin and machine-stitch along the long edge using black thread. Press the seam to the back and pin and machine-stitch each strip to its corresponding window edge.

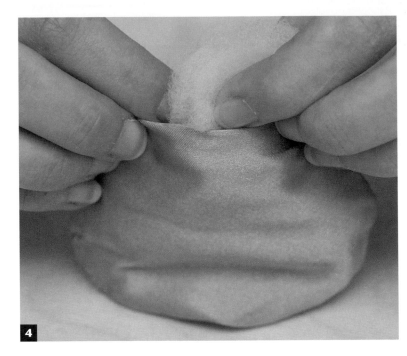

4 From the remaining silver fabric, use a compass and pencil to cut out four 7.5 cm (3 in) diameter circles. Place one on top of another, wrong sides together, pin and machine-stitch with a 12 mm (½ in) hem to make a hub cap. Leave a 2.5 cm (1 in) gap to allow for turning out, and fill with wadding – you need a double-thickness, 5 cm (2 in) circle for each wheel. Hand-stitch to finish, and repeat the process with the two remaining silver circles.

5 From the black fabric, cut out four 27.5 cm (11 in) circles and stitch each pair together, as above, using black thread and leaving a 7.5 cm (3 in) gap to allow for turning. Fill each with single-thickness wadding, measuring 26 cm (10½ in) in diameter. Hand-stitch to finish and sew a single line of stitches around the circumference, 12 mm (½ in) in from the edge.

6 Follow the diagram (see opposite) to assemble the fire engine. Stitch each silver circle to the centre of each black circle to complete the wheels. Pin and machine-stitch each wheel to the bottom of the red panel, using black thread, and stitch around the top half of each one to secure in place. Pin and stitch the yellow panel across the width of the red panel.

7 Pin and machine-stitch the two silver window panels to the upper half of the fire engine. Make a paper template for the flame shape on page 134 and cut out from the leftover yellow fabric. Mark the position of the yellow flame, then pin and machine-stitch in place using yellow thread. Use the yellow embroidery thread to stitch around the edge of the flame for a bolder outline.

8 Cut a total of five square tab tops from the blue and remaining red fabrics, each measuring 17.5 x 17.5 cm (7 x 7 in). Pin and stitch all edges with a 2.5 cm (1 in) hem, using blue and red thread respectively. Pin and machine-stitch each to the top of the wrong side of the red fabric using red thread, 2.5 cm (1 in) deep. Attach 7.5 cm (3 in) strips of hook-and-loop fastener to the back of each tab, one half at the top and the other at the bottom, so that the tabs form a loop around the bed frame.

9 Use a 7.5 x 17.5 cm (3 x 5 in) piece of the blue fabric to make a light for the front of the fire engine. Sew a 12 mm (½ in) hem all round, and stitch to the wrong side of the red panel.

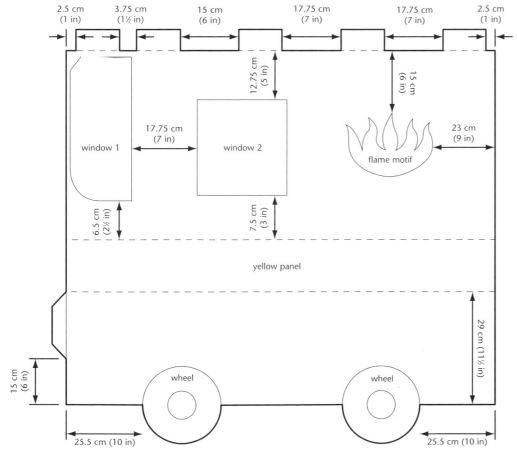

! Top tip

• Measure the width and height of the bed frame before cutting any fabric and keep the stitching as straight as possible.

★ Try this

Adapt the project to make a flap for window 2, rolling it up and securing with ties to keep it open.

In a similar way, you could attach a door panel flap, using hook-and-loop fastener to allow for opening and closing.

See also...

• Goal! Bed, on page 44.

• Picture Height Chart, on page 116.

goal! bed

Quick to complete, this innovative project transforms a raised bed into a real football net. Your child will enjoy helping you paint the 'chalk' markings on the pitch and will relish the chance to practise his penalty-shooting skills in the privacy of his own room.

 easy

 3 hours

 boys

 suitable for a helping hand

you will need

- 700 x 5 cm (280 x 2 in) white carpet tape
- Tape measure
- Scissors
- 400 x 120 cm (160 x 48 in) black net
- 400 x 2.5 cm (160 x 1 in) self-adhesive hook-and-loop fastener
- 200 x 200 cm (80 x 80 in) green felt
- Black felt-tip pen
- Masking tape
- Two A2 sheets of paper
- 30 cm (12 in) round plate or tray
- 25 cm (10 in) round plate or tray
- 125 ml (4 fl oz) white matt emulsion paint
- 5 cm (2 in) paintbrush

1 Make the goal net. Measure and cut 120 cm (48 in) of white carpet tape and peel off the protective film. Lay the tape on the floor and position the edge of one short side of the net along the centre of the tape so that you can fold the other half of the tape over. Press firmly to seal the net in place.

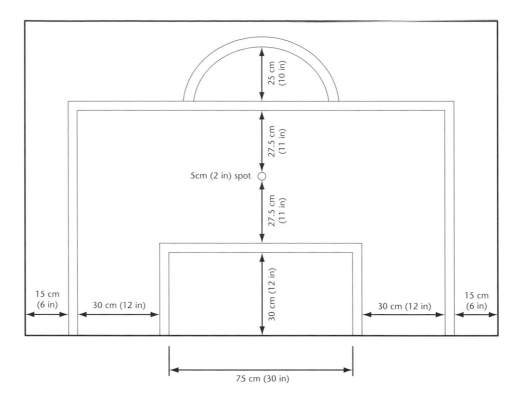

25 cm (10 in)

27.5 cm (11 in)

5cm (2 in) spot ○

27.5 cm (11 in)

30 cm (12 in)

15 cm (6 in)

30 cm (12 in)

30 cm (12 in)

15 cm (6 in)

75 cm (30 in)

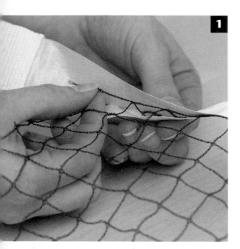

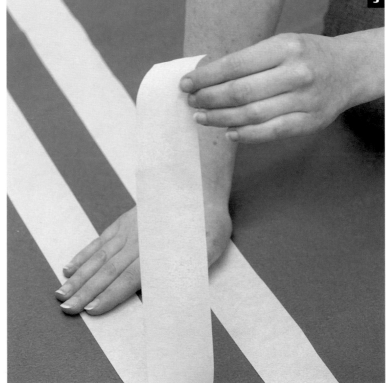

2 Repeat step 1 for the opposite side and one long edge of the net, this time cutting 400 cm (160 in) of carpet tape. Peel and stick one half of the hook-and-loop fastener along the top edge of the net, all the way around. Peel and stick the other half onto the inner frame of the bed. Now attach the net to the bed.

3 Lay the green felt out flat on the floor and follow the diagram (see above) to mark the 4 cm (1½ in) lines for the penalty area in black felt-tip pen (see opposite). Apply masking tape either side of the pen lines to guarantee straight lines.

4 To mark the semi-circles, draw around the 30 cm (12 in) plate or tray on a sheet of paper. Cut out the circle and fold it in half. Repeat with the 25 cm (10 in) plate or tray, leaving you with two semi-circles. Centre the 30 cm (12 in) semi-circle on the horizontal line and draw around it with the felt-tip pen. Position the 25 cm (10 in) semi-circle inside the larger one and draw around it.

5 Paint between the masking tape guides (or pen lines for the semi-circles), using the white paint and 5 cm (2 in) paintbrush. Leave to dry before applying a second coat. Remove the masking tape. When completely dry, position the felt under the bed for play.

! Top tips

• Stretch the net out as much as possible before you start cutting.

• Measure the size of your bed and adjust the measurements for the length and depth of the netting accordingly.

★ Try this

Instead of using white emulsion for the pitch markings, set them out using white carpet tape. This is a particularly good idea if you have wood-laminate flooring, where the green felt can be omitted altogether and the markings made directly on the floor.

See also...

• Football Notice Board, on page 18.

jewelled crown headboard

This elegant, 'jewel'-encrusted headboard is ideal for a princess-themed room. Made to fit a single bed, it is padded for extra comfort, and the velvet-cushion 'jewels' are detachable so they can be moved or scattered on the bed with extra jewel cushions, if desired.

 intermediate

 6 hours

 girls

 not suitable for a helping hand

you will need

- 100 x 90 cm x 18 mm (40 x 36 x ¾ in) MDF panel
- Pencil
- 100 cm (36 in) ruler
- 5 cm (2 in) diameter small cup
- Eraser
- Jigsaw
- Dust mask
- Drill
- 2.5 cm (1 in) drill bit
- Sanding block
- Fine-grade sandpaper
- 150 x 140 x 5 cm (60 x 56 x 2 in) wadding
- Tape measure
- Scissors
- Staple gun
- Fabric:
  150 x 140 cm (60 x 56 in) lilac satin
  50 x 50 cm (20 x 20 in) pink velvet
  50 x 50 cm (20 x 20 in) purple velvet
- Needle
- Tacking thread
- Sewing machine
- Sewing thread:
  Pink
  Purple
- Three 5 x 5 cm (2 x 2 in) self-adhesive hook-and-loop fasteners

1 Draw a crown shape, freehand, on the MDF in pencil. Use a long ruler for the straight edges and a small cup to help with the curves. Erase any lines you are unhappy with. Cut out the shape using a jigsaw. Use a drill to make a 2.5 cm (1 in) hole at the bottom of the inner curves, into which you can guide the jigsaw. Sand all edges smooth.

2 Lay the wadding out flat and place the crown panel on top. Cut around the crown allowing an overlap of 5 cm (2 in).

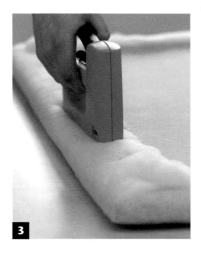

3 Pull the overlap to the back of the MDF shape and staple 2.5 cm (1 in) in from the edge. Trim any excess wadding to 6 mm (¼ in) from the staples.

4 Lay the lilac satin flat, wrong side up, and place the crown panel over the top, with the wadding face down. Cut around the crown allowing an overlap of 5 cm (2 in) along the bottom and side edges, and 10 cm (4 in) across the top.

5 Starting at the bottom, lift the fabric and tuck it under the loose edge of wadding, stapling as close to the edge of the fabric as possible. Now work the top of the crown. Cut vertical lines from the top of the fabric down to the centre of each curve, stopping 5 cm (2 in) short. Lift, tuck and staple the fabric as above, pulling it tight. Now work down both the straight sides.

6 Cut two 100 x 7.5 cm (40 x 3 in) lengths from the excess lilac satin and two 95 x 5 cm (38 x 2 in) lengths from the excess wadding. Centre each length of the wadding on a length of fabric, fold the edges of the fabric over and lightly tack together to make a tube. Position the first tube across the front of the crown, just below the shaped top and staple each end to the back of the MDF. Attach the second tube in the same way, 20 cm (8 in) below the first.

7 Use the velvet fabrics to make small scatter cushions. For each of the square cushions, cut two 15 x 15 cm (6 x 6 in) squares and place one on top of the other, right sides together. Machine-stitch all four sides, leaving a 5 cm (2 in) opening for inserting wadding for a plump finish. Hand-stitch to finish. For a rectangular cushion, cut out two 30 x 25 cm (12 x 10 in) rectangles and complete in the same way.

8 For each scatter cushion stick one half of the hook-and-loop fastener to the cushion and the other half to the crown.

 Top tips

• When cutting around the crown on the wadding and lilac fabric, make sure you position the MDF well, leaving enough excess material to complete the remaining steps.

• This project works best with a stretchy fabric, so that you can work the material around the curves at the top of the crown to give a much smoother finish with few creases.

★ Try this

Weave a feather boa through the top of the crown for a luxurious finishing touch.

Instead of using hook-and-loop fasteners, make a buttonhole in one corner of each cushion and sew a matching-coloured button onto the headboard.

See also...

• Pretty Pocket Bed Throw, on page 52.

• Domino Toy Boxes, on page 82.

pretty pocket bed throw

This is a very simple, yet effective design for giving an old bed throw a new look. A row of pockets sewn down each side of the throw provides the perfect place for keeping a child's favourite dolls, toys and books, making bedtime more fun.

you will need

- 195 x 60 cm (78 x 24 in) patterned pink gingham fabric
- Scissors
- Sewing pins
- Sewing machine
- Pink sewing thread
- 190 x 120 cm (76 x 48 in) pink bed throw
- Needle
- Tacking thread
- Tape measure

 easy

 4 hours

 girls

 not suitable for a helping hand

1 Cut the gingham fabric in half lengthways, to make two panels measuring 195 x 30 cm (78 x 12 in). Pin and hem all sides of each panel by 2.5 cm (1 in).

2 Position and tack each panel along one long edge of the bed throw, keeping the fabric as flat as possible.

3 Machine-stitch the outside edges of the throw to secure.

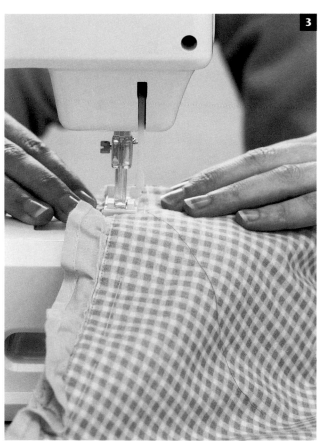

4 Use a tape measure to divide the length of each panel into pockets approximately 24 cm (9½ in) wide, pinning to mark the divisions. Stitch along each one to secure.

⚠ **Top tips**

• Although you can hand-stitch each pocket, a sewing machine will provide a much stronger and more durable stitch.

• Use remnants of the curtain fabric in your child's room to tie the bed throw into an overall scheme.

★ **Try this**

Stitch a number of pockets randomly on to the bed throw, running across the middle or even in a circle.

See also...

• Drop-leaf Flower Desk, on page 10.

• Jewelled Crown Headboard, on page 48.

• Butterfly Handles, on page 112.

jigsaw cushions

Use these two jigsaw shapes to make any number of interlocking pastel cushions. They are ideal in a nursery, as soft cushions for a baby to rest on, or for a toddler who is learning to piece simple jigsaws together for the first time.

 intermediate

 6 hours

 girls and boys

 not suitable for a helping hand

you will need

- Two 30 x 30 cm (12 x 12 in) sheets of paper for templates (see Templates, page 132)
- Scissors
- Fabric:
  100 x 50 cm (40 x 20 in) cream fleece
  100 x 50 cm (40 x 20 in) baby pink fleece
  100 x 50 cm (40 x 20 in) baby blue fleece
  100 x 50 cm (40 x 20 in) pastel green fleece
- Pen

- Sewing pins
- Tape measure
- Needle
- Tacking thread
- Sewing machine
- Sewing thread:
  Cream
  Baby pink
  Baby blue
  Pastel green
- 200 x 100 x 5 cm (80 x 40 x 2 in) fire-retardant wadding

1 Enlarge each jigsaw pattern on page 135 to make two 27.5 x 27.5 cm (10 x 10 in) templates and cut out. Select two different-coloured fabrics for each shape.

2 To make a cushion, first fold the fabric in half and pin the template on top, aligning the corner of the template with one corner of the fabric. Draw around the template and cut out to give you the top and bottom of the jigsaw cushion.

2

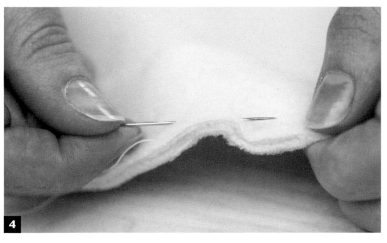

4

5

3 To make the side panels of each cushion, cut two 5 cm (2 in) wide strips from the remaining fabric. You need approximately 120 cm (48 in) length in total, but measure your jigsaw panel shape for accuracy.

4 Pin and tack the strips of fabric around the perimeter of the first jigsaw panel, wrong sides together, taking a 12 mm (½ in) seam and joining the short ends as you go. Now tack the strip to the second jigsaw panel in the same way. Machine-stitch in place, leaving a 7.5 cm (3 in) opening to allow for turning the cushion the right way out.

6

5 Turn the cushion the right way out and fill with wadding, making sure that all corners and curves are filled adequately. Fill the cushion to a depth of 2.5 cm (1 in).

6 Hand-stitch the opening to close. Repeat the process to make the remaining three cushions.

 Top tip

• Whatever filling you choose for the cushions, be sure to use one that is fire retardant.

★ Try this

Use eight different-coloured fabrics so that each cushion has a different colour on each side. Use bright red, yellow, green and blue – a great way for a young child to learn basic colours.

Make little jigsaw seat cushions by using foam instead of wadding.

See also...

• Jigsaw Wall Art, on page 26.

bird cot mobile

This pretty mobile uses simple, sunshine shapes – ideal for brightening up a baby's nursery. This is a great project to make with an older child in preparation for the imminent arrival of a new sibling. Encourage him or her to help you stuff the felt shapes.

intermediate

5 hours

girls and boys

suitable for a
helping hand

you will need

- 40 x 30 cm (16 x 12 in) card for
  templates (see Templates, page 132)
- Scissors
- Glue
- Felt:
  50 x 50 cm (20 x 20 in) white
  Eight 25 x 25 cm (10 x 10 in) sky blue
  10 x 10 cm (4 x 4 in) orange
  50 x 50 cm (20 x 20 in) yellow
- Fine black felt-tip pen
- Needle

- Sewing thread:
  White
  Blue
  Yellow
- 50 x 2.5 cm (20 x 1 in) wadding
- 305 cm x 5 mm (122 x ⅜ in) blue satin
  cord
- 40 x 40 cm (16 x 16 in) cardboard
- 35 cm (14 in) diameter plate
- Sewing machine
- Glue gun
- Screw hook

1 Start by making card templates of the four shapes on page 136.

2 Folding each piece of felt in half – so that you cut two shapes each time – use a felt-tip pen to draw and cut the following number of shapes: five clouds and eight cloud edges from the white felt; three bird bodies and four bird wings from the blue felt; seven bird beaks and one sun circle from the orange felt; four bird bodies, three bird wings and one set of sunrays from the yellow felt.

3 Start to assemble the mobile pieces. Using white thread, hand-stitch two pieces of cloud together leaving a 5 mm (⅛ in) gap centred at both the top and bottom for the cord. Leave an additional 2.5 cm (1 in) gap on the side, fill the cloud with wadding and hand-stitch the gap to finish. Complete each of the five clouds in the same way.

4 Assemble each bird, stitching on the wings and beaks, and complete in the same way as the clouds, leaving a 5 mm (⅛ in) gap top and bottom, and using the same-colour sewing threads. Repeat the process for making the sun, stitching the sunrays between the two orange circles. Leave a 5 mm (⅛ in) gap at the top only and fill with wadding.

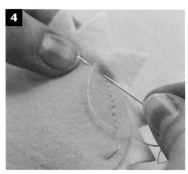

5 Cut the blue cord into six 5 cm (2 in) lengths, six 10 cm (4 in) lengths and one 15 cm (6 in) length. Tuck one end of the 15 cm (6 in) cord into the gap at the top of the sun and stitch in place.

6 Decide on the arrangement of birds and clouds for the mobiles – three shapes on each. Take a length of cord, tuck it into the gap at the top of the first shape and stitch in place using blue thread. Tuck one end of a second length of cord into the bottom of this shape and stitch, then tuck the other end into the top of the second shape and stitch, then attach the last shape. Repeat for the remaining mobiles, alternating the lengths of cord.

7 To make the sky, machine-stitch four pieces of blue felt together to make a large square, using blue thread and taking a 6 mm (¼ in) seam. Repeat with the remaining pieces of felt. Lay one square on top of the other. Cut a circle from card, drawing around the plate, and place on top of the felt squares. Cut out a circle with a 12 mm (½ in) hem. Sandwich the card between the felt, wrong sides together. Machine-stitch the felt, trimming any excess.

8 Attach the sun to the centre of one side of the sky by pushing the end of the cord through at the point where all stitches meet and stitching in place. Stitch the remaining cord lengths to the sky, one at the end of each seam. Stitch five 30 cm (12 in) lengths of cord to the opposite side of the sky in the same positions, and tie the loose ends together at the top, making sure the lengths are equal. Stitch the knot to secure.

9 Using the glue gun, glue each white cloud edge to the outside edge of the sky, overlapping them slightly as you work round. Fix a screw hook to the ceiling where desired and hang the mobile.

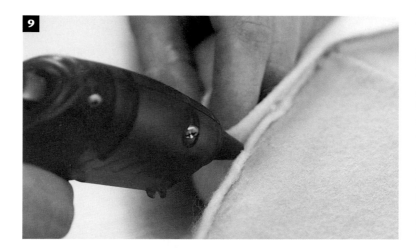

 Top tips

• When cutting the felt shapes, you may wish to draw all of the shapes for one colour before cutting out, to make sure you have the best fit.

• Measure the height of your ceiling and adjust the cord lengths to suit.

• You can make the sky section of the mobile from one piece of felt, but you will need to measure and mark out the positions for hanging the cords.

★ **Try this**

Make a mobile with a night-time theme, replacing the clouds with white stars, the birds with yellow and orange planets, and the sun with a striking crescent moon. Use a deeper blue felt for the sky.

See also...
• Pocket Cot Tidy, on page 70.
• Nursery Wall Frieze, on page 120.

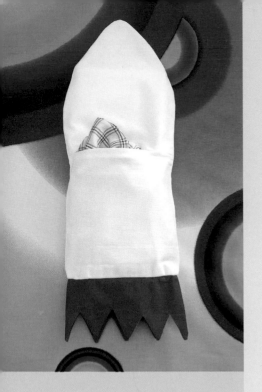

rocket pyjama case

This rocket-shaped pyjama case is a simple sewing project that can be completed easily in a weekend. Adapt the design by adding different details to the front, then attach a hook to the back of the rocket so that your child can hang it up and 'launch' it during the day.

 intermediate

 8 hours

 boys

 not suitable for a helping hand

you will need

- Fabric:
  50 x 100 cm (20 x 40 in)
    white cotton
  25 x 25 cm (10 x 10 in)
    yellow cotton
  40 x 2.5 cm (16 x 1 in)
    green cotton
  50 x 50 cm (20 x 20 in)
    red cotton
- Tape measure
- Scissors
- 15 cm (6 in) white zip
- Sewing pins
- Sewing machine

- Sewing thread:
  White
  Black
  Green
  Red
- 25 x 5 cm (10 x 2 in) bonding web
- Iron and board
- 30 x 12 mm (12 x ½ in)
    red ribbon
- 30 x 40 cm (12 x 16 in) sheet of paper
    for templates (see Templates,
      page 132)

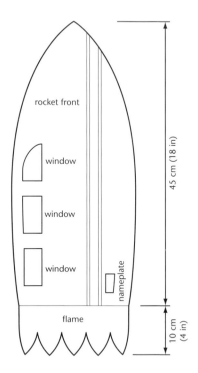

rocket front

window

window

window

nameplate

flame

45 cm (18 in)

10 cm (4 in)

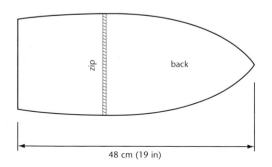

zip

back

48 cm (19 in)

1 Follow the illustration (see left) to cut out two 'rocket' shapes from the white fabric (not including the flame base). Note that the second rocket needs to be 3 cm (1¼ in) longer than the first. Cut the longer panel in half across the width, then pin and machine-stitch the zip to the cut edges using white thread.

2 Cut three 2.5 x 4 cm (1 x 1½ in) yellow rectangles and three pieces of bonding web 6 mm (⅛ in) smaller all round. Centre on a yellow rectangle. Fold the edges of the yellow fabric over the bonding web and iron in place on the rocket. Secure by hand using black thread. Repeat with the remaining rectangles, shaping one for the top window, if wished. Attach a smaller yellow rectangle in the same way, for the rocket's nameplate.

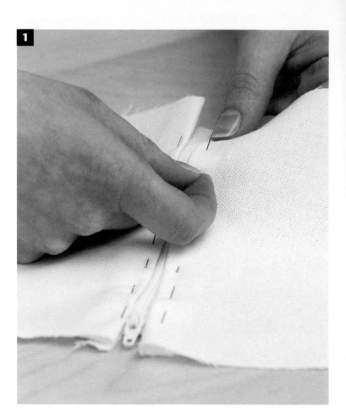

3 Take the green strip of fabric and fold both long edges in to the middle to make a 12 mm (½ in) wide strip. Pin and machine-stitch to the rocket with green thread. Attach the strip of red ribbon in the same way using red thread.

4 Use the flame template on page 137 to cut four shapes from the red fabric, allowing a 12 mm (½ in) seam. Lay two flames wrong sides together and stitch a 12 mm (½ in) seam along the zigzag edges. Repeat with the second pair of flames.

5 Open out each pair of stitched flames. Pin and machine-stitch them to each other along the short edges, to form a circle. Trim back the seam allowance, turn the flames right side out and iron flat, making sure all of the points are true.

6 Using white thread, stitch the front and back of the rocket, right sides together, along the two long sides and nose, neatening the edge with zigzag stitch. Turn right side out and stitch the flame section to the bottom of the rocket, taking a 12 mm (½ in) seam allowance, and sewing carefully for a neat and accurate finish.

7 Make a template of the base of the rocket using the shape on page 137 and cut out the base from what remains of the red fabric. Pin and machine-stitch this to the bottom of the rocket, along the inside seam with the flames, trimming off all loose threads.

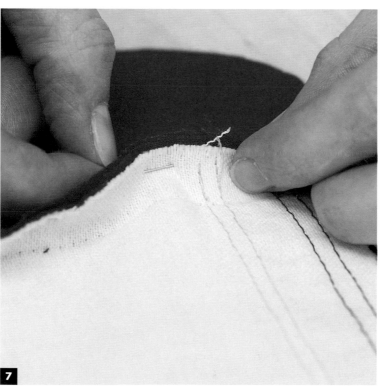

! Top tip

• Cut out the pieces of fabric in advance, where possible, and always add a little extra. You can trim off excess fabric later.

★ Try this

Make a planet pyjama case by cutting out two circles and inserting a zip when stitching together. Decorate with fabric paint to look like a planet's surface.

See also...

• Rocket Lamp, on page 98.

• Star and Moon Blind, on page 124.

storage and
lighting

pocket cot tidy

A useful addition to the nursery, this tidy attaches neatly to the side of a cot and provides a handy place to keep all your baby essentials – rattles, creams and cotton wool. The drawstring bags are detachable, which means they are easily carried around the house or on outings.

intermediate

5 hours

girls and boys

not suitable for
a helping hand

you will need

- Fabric:
  150 x 140 cm (60 x 56 in)
    white canvas
  60 x 60 cm (24 x 24 in)
    yellow gingham
  60 x 60 cm (24 x 24 in)
    yellow-spotted cotton
  35 x 30 cm (14 x 12 in)
    multi-spotted yellow cotton
  85 x 60 cm (34 x 24 in)
    cream lining fabric
- Tape measure
- Scissors
- Sewing machine
- Sewing thread:
  White
  Yellow
- 83 x 63 cm (33½ x 25½ in) wadding
- Sewing pins
- Four buttons
- Iron and board
- 120 cm x 6 mm (48 x ¼ in)
    yellow ribbon
- 120 cm x 6 mm (48 x ¼ in)
    white ribbon
- Safety pin
- 15 press studs

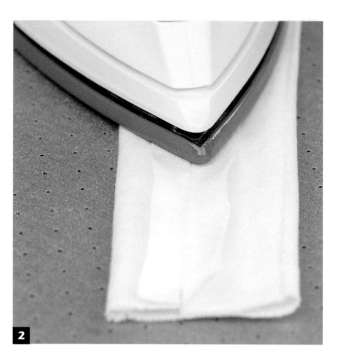

1 Measure and cut the white fabric. You need two 83 x 63 cm (33½ x 25½ in) panels and four 30 x 15 cm (12 x 6 in) rectangles for the tabs.

2 Fold each tab in half lengthways, wrong sides together, pin and machine-stitch using white thread and taking a 12 mm (½ in) seam. Open the seam and press so that the seam is in the middle of the tab. Stitch across one end of the tab with a 5 mm (⅛ in) hem and turn right side out. Make a buttonhole at the closed end of the tab.

3 Assemble the background panel (see below). Lay the wadding out flat on the floor and centre one white panel on top, right side up. Align the unsewn end of each of the four tabs with the top edge of the white panel, flat and at 12.5 cm (5 in) intervals from one another, with two tabs positioned 6 cm (2½ in) in from the edges. Place the second white panel on top, wrong side up. Pin all pieces together across the top and down both sides, taking a 12 mm (½ in) seam, and machine-stitch. Turn the whole assembly right side out from the open end, turn a 12 mm (½ in) hem along the bottom edge and slip-stitch to finish. Fold the four tabs to the front and use as a guide to position and sew on the buttons.

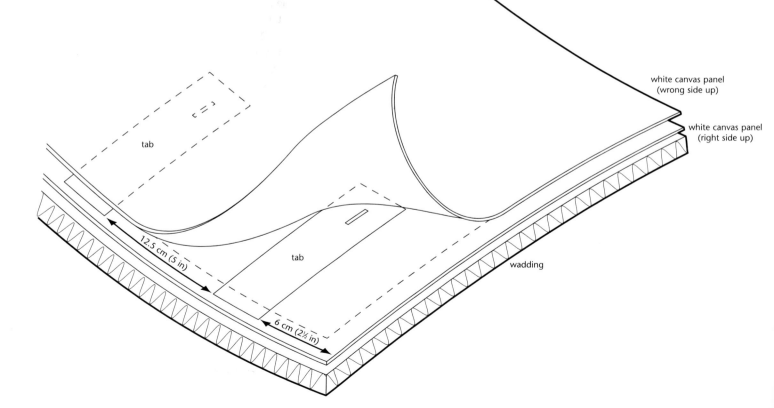

tab

white canvas panel
(wrong side up)

white canvas panel
(right side up)

12.5 cm (5 in)

tab

wadding

6 cm (2½ in)

4 Now make the drawstring pockets. From the yellow fabrics, cut material for three small bags, measuring 33 x 26.5 cm (13 x 10½ in) and two large bags measuring 53 x 31.5 cm (21 x 12½ in) each. From the lining fabric, cut three pieces measuring 33 x 18 cm (13 x 7 in) and two measuring 53 x 23 cm (21 x 9 in).

5 For each bag, pin and machine-stitch the yellow fabric and corresponding lining along one long edge, right sides together, taking a 6 mm (¼ in) seam and using yellow thread. Open out and press the seam towards the lining. With the seam running from left to right in front of you, make a small buttonhole halfway across the width of the fabric, and 7 cm (2¾ in) down from the seam.

6 Now fold the fabric in half lengthways, right sides together, still with the sewn seam running from left to right. Pin and machine-stitch the long edge, taking a 6 mm (¼ in) seam. Press this seam open to the centre of the tube you have made. (The seam is now at the back of the bag and the buttonhole at the front.)

7 Pin and machine-stitch the bottom edge of the yellow fabric and turn right side out. Press under a 12 mm (½ in) seam on the bottom of the lining fabric and stitch close to the edge so that the inside of the bag is neat with no raw edges showing. Push the lining into the bag and press, making sure the seams are flat.

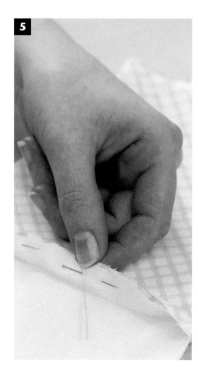

8 Machine a line of stitching below the buttonhole and a second line above the buttonhole so that you have a channel 12 mm (½ in) wide through which to feed the ribbon. You will need 40 cm (16 in) lengths of yellow for the small bags and 60 cm (24 in) lengths of white for the large bags. Use a safety pin to feed in the ribbon and tie a knot in each end to stop the ribbon slipping out. Repeat steps 5 to 8 to make the remaining four bags.

9 Sew the halves of three press-studs onto the back of each bag: one centre top and one in each corner. Position the bags on the background, so that you have three at the top and two at the bottom. When happy with the layout, sew the matching halves of the press-studs into place. Attach the bags and hang the tidy on the cot.

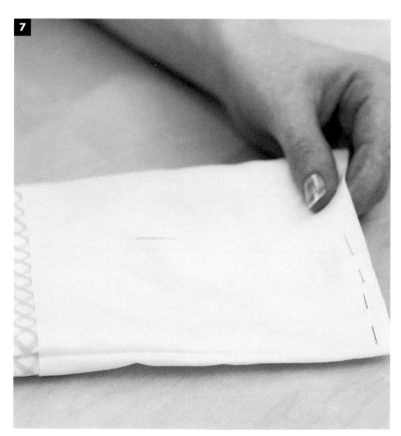

 Top tip

• Make the bags from remnants of the curtain fabric in your child's room to tie everything into an overall scheme.

★ Try this

Instead of having a rectangular shape for the cot tidy panel, make one the same shape as the bags. Shape it to look as if it has been half-drawn at the top, with ribbon hanging down to complete the look.

See also...
• Bird Cot Mobile, on page 60.
• Nursery Wall Frieze, on page 120.

rainforest storage

A useful addition to a room with a rainforest theme, see also pages 90 and 108, this stylish storage unit provides plenty of space to keep all sorts of toys and games. The addition of a simple curtain across the front means that everything can be hidden away to keep the room tidy.

advanced

9 hours

girls and boys

not suitable for a helping hand

you will need

- Two 100 x 80 cm x 12 mm (39⅜ x 31½ x ½ in) MDF panels for front and back
- Two 61 x 37.5 cm x 12 mm (24 x 14¾ x ½ in) MDF panels for the ends
- Two 77.5 x 37.5 cm x 12 mm (30½ x 14¾ x ½ in) MDF panels for intermediate uprights
- Three 37.2 x 31.5 cm x 12 mm (14⅝ x 12⅜ x ½ in) MDF panels for the shelves
- Six 37.5 x 1.5 x 1.5 cm (14¾ x ⅝ x ⅝ in) softwood shelf supports
- One 100 x 40 cm x 3 mm (39⅜ x 15¾ x ⅛ in) sheet hardboard for the bottom
- One 110 x 40 cm x 3 mm (43⅜ x 15¾ x ⅛ in) sheet hardboard for the top
- Hammer
- 2.5 cm (1 in) panel pins
- Tape measure
- Pencil
- 110 cm (45 in) string
- G-cramps
- Jigsaw

- Dust mask
- Drill and 10-mm drill bit
- Plane and sanding block
- Medium-grade sandpaper
- PVA glue
- Pin punch
- Matt emulsion paint:
  500 ml (17 fl oz) light green
  250 ml (8 fl oz) dark green
  250 ml (8 fl oz) brown
  125 ml (4 fl oz) yellow
  125 ml (4 fl oz) blue
- 4 cm (1½ in) paintbrush and paint tray
- 70 x 90 cm (28 x 36 in) thick green cotton fabric
- Scissors
- 30 x 40 cm (12 x 16 in) sheet acetate for stencils (see Templates, page 132)
- Black felt-tip pen
- Craft knife and cutting mat
- Fabric paint:
  125 ml (4 fl oz) red
  125 ml (4 fl oz) blue
  125 ml (4 fl oz) purple
- 12 mm (½ in) paintbrush
- Staple gun

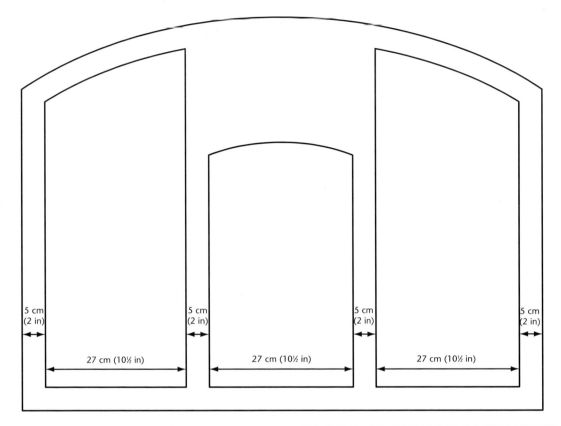

5 cm (2 in)

5 cm (2 in)

5 cm (2 in)

5 cm (2 in)

27 cm (10½ in)

27 cm (10½ in)

27 cm (10½ in)

1 Take the front and back MDF panels and lay them flat on top of each other. Temporarily pin them together with panel pins, leaving the pinheads protruding for easy removal later. Measure and mark 1 cm (⅜ in) up from the bottom of the panel and 50 cm (19⅝ in) in from the left edge. This identifies the compass point for marking the three curves required.

2 Make a basic compass by tying the pencil 99 cm (39 in) along one end of the piece of string. Holding the opposite end at your compass point, pull the string taught and draw an arc across the MDF with the pencil. Use the same method to draw an arc with the pencil at 94 cm (37 in) along the piece of string, and another at 76 cm (30 in) along the piece of string.

3 Secure the two panels to a bench using G-clamps and use the jigsaw to cut the top curve on both panels Remove the pins holding them together and set the back panel aside.

4 Follow the diagram (see above) to measure and mark the three openings on the front panel, using the width measurements given, and taking the height to where each line meets the drawn arcs, so that you have two tall panels left and right, and a short panel in the centre. Draw in all the lines clearly for cutting.

5 Drill a hole, inside the lines, in each corner of the required openings – 12 holes in total – to enable access for your jigsaw blade. Carefully cut along the lines with your jigsaw. When you have cut out all three openings, plane and sand all edges smooth.

5

6 Measure and mark 29 cm (11½ in) up from the bottom on one side of each end panel. Glue and pin on one of the shelf supports using panel pins for each end panel. For the two intermediate upright panels, measure and mark the same distance on both sides of each, then glue and pin on the shelf supports.

7 Attach each of the end panels to the back of the front panel, the long edges flush with each other. Secure by gluing and pinning through the front panel. Attach the two intermediate upright panels in the same way, at equal distances from the end panels. Position, glue and fix the back panel. Glue and pin on the hardboard base. Position and fix the hardboard top. Sand any sharp edges and allow the glue to dry overnight.

8 Tap the pinheads below the surface by using a pin-punch. Lay the shelves onto the shelf supports, trimming to fit if required.

9 Paint the whole storage unit using light green emulsion paint and the 4 cm (1½ in) paintbrush and leave to dry. Draw your rainforest design in pencil then paint using emulsion.

10 To make the fabric blinds, measure and cut two 70 x 30 cm (28 x 12 in) lengths of the dark green fabric for the side openings and one 52 x 30 cm (21 x 12 in) length for the middle opening.

11 Make acetate stencils of the shapes on page 138 and use these to paint, randomly, the leaves, stems and flower details using different-coloured fabric paints and the 12 mm (½ in) paintbrush. Leave the blinds to dry before stapling each to the inside of its respective opening of the storage unit.

 Top tip

• It is a good idea to fix the shelves to prevent the possibility of an accident. Spread some glue onto the shelf battens before positioning the shelves, and leave the glue to dry.

★ **Try this**

Attach some brown, straw-like rope to the top of the unit so that you can roll the blinds up during play.

See also...

• Sunflower Nightlight, on page 90.

• Tiger Tie-backs, on page 108.

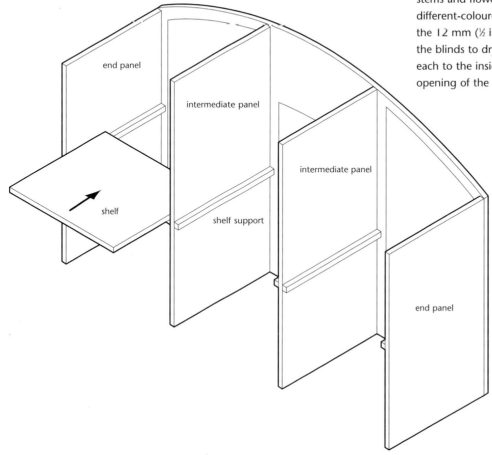

end panel

intermediate panel

shelf

intermediate panel

shelf support

end panel

CD screen

This is a great project for a teenager's room, offering a novel way to show off CDs. Your child can help you to put it together, arranging the discs by band name, if they like. All CD inlays can be removed, so changes to the collection can be made by swapping the disc and inlay.

 intermediate

 6 hours

 boys

 suitable for a helping hand

you will need

- Three 150 x 40 cm x 12 mm (60 x 16 x ½ in) MDF panels
- Sanding block
- Fine-grade sandpaper
- 500 ml (17 fl oz) silver paint
- 5 cm (2 in) paintbrush
- Six 2.5 x 2.5 cm (1 x 1 in) hinges with screws
- Screwdriver
- Pencil
- 100 cm (36 in) ruler
- 54 CDs
- 10 x 8 cm (4 x 3½ in) card for template (see Templates, page 132)
- Glue gun

1 Sand the edges of all three MDF panels until smooth. Brush away the dust and paint all surfaces silver. Leave to dry.

2 Fix three hinges to the long edge of one panel, one at the centre and one each at 10 cm (4 in) from top and bottom respectively. Join the second panel to the first, aligning them properly, and join the third panel to the second in the same way.

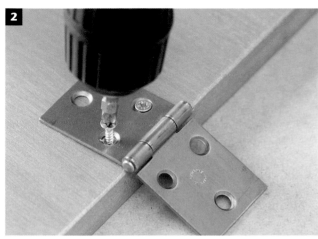

3 Use a pencil and the long ruler to mark out a 5 cm (2 in) frame around each panel. Take the first CD and glue it in the top left-hand corner of the frame. Make a card template of the 'spacer' on page 135 and use this to determine the positions of the remaining CDs for that panel. Abut the spacer to the bottom right-hand corner of the first CD, then mark the position of the CD to the right of it, and the two below. Glue these three CDs into place.

4 Abut the spacer to the bottom corners of the last two CDs to mark the positions of the next two, and so on. Glue each pair in place before moving on.

5 Repeat steps 3 and 4 to fill all three panels.

(!) Top tips

• Ask your timber merchant to cut the three MDF panels to size for you. This will save time and make the project easier to complete.

• Be sure to buy hinges complete with screw fittings.

★ Try this

Use the same technique to make a screen to house a large collection of DVDs or computer games.

See also...

• Noughts and Crosses Cushion, on page 22.

domino toy boxes

A quick-and-easy project for giving plain storage boxes a new lease of life. Your child will enjoy helping you to sponge on the dots, and you could even make more boxes for a giant game of dominoes. Simply change the colours for a boy's room if desired.

easy

3 hours

girls

suitable for a
helping hand

you will need

- Three 40 x 30 x 23 cm
  (15¾ x 11¾ x 9 in) pine boxes
- 250 ml (8 fl oz) wood primer
- 5 cm (2 in) paintbrush
- Matt emulsion paint:
  250 ml (8 fl oz) lilac
  125 ml (4 fl oz) purple
- Pencil
- Ruler
- 12 mm (½ in) paintbrush
- Paint tray
- 5 cm (2 in) diameter circle sponge
- Kitchen paper
- 250 ml (8 fl oz) clear satin varnish

Top tip

• If you do not want to varnish the boxes, use a satinwood or soft-sheen paint for a wipe-clean surface.

1 Prime all three boxes using the 5 cm (2 in) paintbrush. When dry, use the lilac emulsion to paint the boxes inside and out. Leave to dry completely.

2 For each box, use a pencil and ruler to draw a vertical line down the centre of one long side (starting and stopping short of the top and bottom edges), and paint over using purple paint and the 12 mm (½ in) paintbrush.

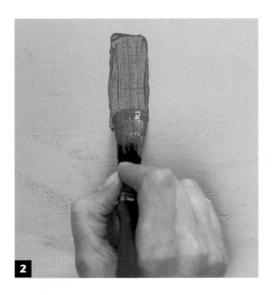

★ **Try this**

Attach self-adhesive magnets to the short ends of each box so that they can actually be used for a game of dominoes.

Use a star- or flower-shaped sponge to make the dots to match a room theme.

See also...

• Noughts and Crosses Cushion, on page 22.
• Jewelled Crown Headboard, on page 48.

3 Pour some purple paint into a paint tray and press the round sponge into it. Dab off any excess paint onto some kitchen paper and press lightly for each spot onto the boxes: box 1 has one spot on the left and two on the right; box 2 has two spots on the left and three on the right; box 3 has three spots on the left and one on the right.

4 Once all the paint is dry, give each box a coat of varnish, inside and out, using the 5 cm (2 in) paintbrush.

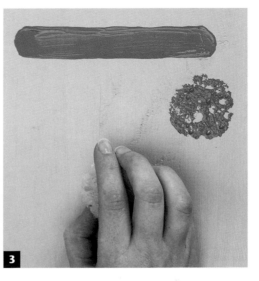

pot of gold nightlight

This unique nightlight makes a perfect finishing touch to a room with a rainbow theme (see also Rainbow Curtain, page 36). The light looks fantastic both day and night with its piles of glistening gold coins, and you and your child can have fun making it together.

 intermediate

 3 hours

 girls and boys

 suitable for a helping hand

you will need

- 30 x 30 cm (12 x 12 in) plastic plant pot (30 cm/12 in diameter at top)
- Tape measure
- 50 x 50 cm x 3 mm (20 x 20 x ⅛ in) MDF panel
- Compass
- Pencil
- Jigsaw
- Dust mask
- Sanding block
- Fine-grade sandpaper
- PVA glue
- Drill
- 2.5 cm (1 in) drill bit
- 12 mm (½ in) drill bit
- 30 x 30 cm (12 x 12 in) card
- Scissors
- Plastic coins (approximately 100)
- Gold spray paint
- Light fitting
- Glue gun
- Screwdriver
- Maximum 40 watt light bulb

1 Make a lid for the plant pot. Measure the diameter inside the pot 12 mm (½ in) down from the top and transfer this size to the MDF using a compass and pencil. Cut out the circle using a jigsaw. Cut out three additional MDF circles with 22.5 cm (9 in), 17.5 cm (7 in) and 7.5 cm (3 in) diameters and sand all edges smooth. Glue the circles in a stack, centred on one another from largest to smallest and leave to dry.

2 Drill a 2.5 cm (1 in) hole, 2.5 cm (1 in) up from the bottom of the pot. When the lid is dry, and still using the 2.5 cm (1 in) drill bit, drill a finger hole at each side of the largest circle to allow for easy placing and removing of the lid. Now use the 12 mm (½ in) drill bit to drill approximately twenty holes into the MDF at random. Sand all holes until smooth.

3 Cut out at least thirty 'coin' circles from the cardboard and glue them to the MDF lid using PVA glue and trying not to cover any of the drilled holes. Build them up to look like piles of money, now glue on the plastic coins individually, and leave to dry.

4 Meanwhile spray-paint the outside and at least the top half of the inside of the plant pot in gold. Spray-paint the lid.

5 When the pot is dry, use the glue gun to secure the light fitting to the base of the pot. Having removed the plug, feed the cable through the pre-drilled hole at the side of the pot. Re-attach the plug. Fit the bulb and position the coin lid over the top.

! **Top tips**

• Drill as many holes in the lid as you need. Try putting the light on in the dark as you work to see if you have the right amount of light coming through.

• Always use a low-wattage bulb. If you want to have more light shining through just drill a few more small holes at random.

• If you find you have too much light coming through, cover some of the holes with coins.

★ **Try this**
Make a treasure chest light in the same way. Simply dress up the lid with beaded necklaces and bracelets in all colours – perfect for a princess theme or a pirate's den.

See also...
• Rainbow Curtain, on page 36.

pot of gold nightlight   **89**

sunflower nightlight

This simple design for a flower nightlight can easily be adapted to a room with a garden, jungle or forest theme – just change the colour of the flowerhead to suit. Your child can enjoy making it with you – positioning and gluing the leaves and attaching the flower to the wall.

easy

2 hours

girls and boys

suitable for a
helping hand

you will need

- Two 40 x 30 cm (16 x 12 in) sheets
  card for templates (see Templates,
    page 132)
- Scissors
- Felt:
  50 x 50 cm (20 x 20 in) green
  50 x 50 cm (20 x 20 in) yellow
- Sewing pins
- PVA glue
- Touch light (battery-operated)
- Pencil
- Six 2.5 cm (1 in) double-sided adhesive
    foam pads

1 Start by making card templates of the sunflower, stem and three leaf shapes on page 140.

2 Fold the green felt in half, pin the stem template to it and cut out the shape carefully to give you two identical stems. Repeat the process with the leaf templates, to leave you with six leaves in total.

3 Lay one stem out flat and glue one of each leaf size as follows, using the template on page 140 as a guide: the smallest 2.5 cm (1 in) up from the bottom of the stem, on the right-hand side; the medium leaf 7.5 cm (3 in) above the smallest; and the largest leaf on the left, 2.5 cm (1 in) up from the bottom.

4 Glue the second stem and each of the second leaf shapes on top of the first. Cut one more large leaf shape from the remaining felt, trim in half lengthways and glue to the centre of the large leaf.

5 Fold the yellow felt in half and use the card template to cut out the flower shape. Glue the two flower shapes together, having first positioned the green stem 2.5 cm (1 in) in at the bottom, between the two layers of yellow felt.

6 Place the touch light centrally on the front of the flower and mark its position with a pencil, flip the flower over and do the same on the back.

7 Still working on the back of the flower, remove the battery cover and carefully transfer its position to the yellow felt, then cut out this panel through both pieces of felt. If the light has a hook for wall-mounting, mark and cut a hole in the felt for this as well.

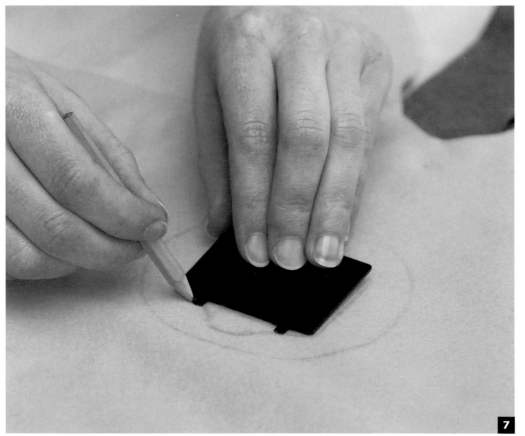

8

8 Now turn the flower back over to the front and glue the light in place. Place the flower face down once more to make sure you are able to remove the battery cover with ease, trimming the felt if necessary. Attach the self-adhesive foam pads – two running up the stem and four at equal distances around the perimeter of the flower head, and stick the nightlight to the wall.

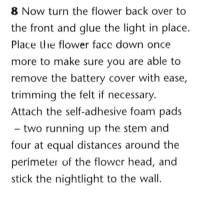

⚠ **Top tips**

• If drawing the flower directly onto the felt freehand, make sure you draw on the wrong side so that you are not left with visible pen marks.

• If the touch light has a hook for fixing it to the wall, you can use this to hang the light instead of foam pads.

★ **Try this**

Use the same idea to make a car light, drawing the side view of a car and using two touch lights for the wheels – great for a transport theme.

See also...

• Rainforest Storage, on page 74.

• Tiger Tie-backs, on page 108.

sunflower nightlight   **93**

pretty voile pockets

These pretty bags offer a quick-and-easy way to brighten up a bedroom wall or dressing table. Filled with a girl's favourite jewellery and hair accessories, the simple organza bags will glisten, with all of the rich colours shining through.

you will need

- 65 x 30 cm (26 x 12 in) white organza
- Tape measure
- Scissors
- Sewing pins
- Sewing machine
- White sewing thread
- 50 cm (20 in) medium-weight coated wire
- Wire cutters
- 150 cm x 18 mm (60 x ¾ in) red gingham ribbon
- Fabric glue
- 8.75 x 3.75 cm (3½ x 1½ in) red card

intermediate

3 hours

girls

not suitable for a helping hand

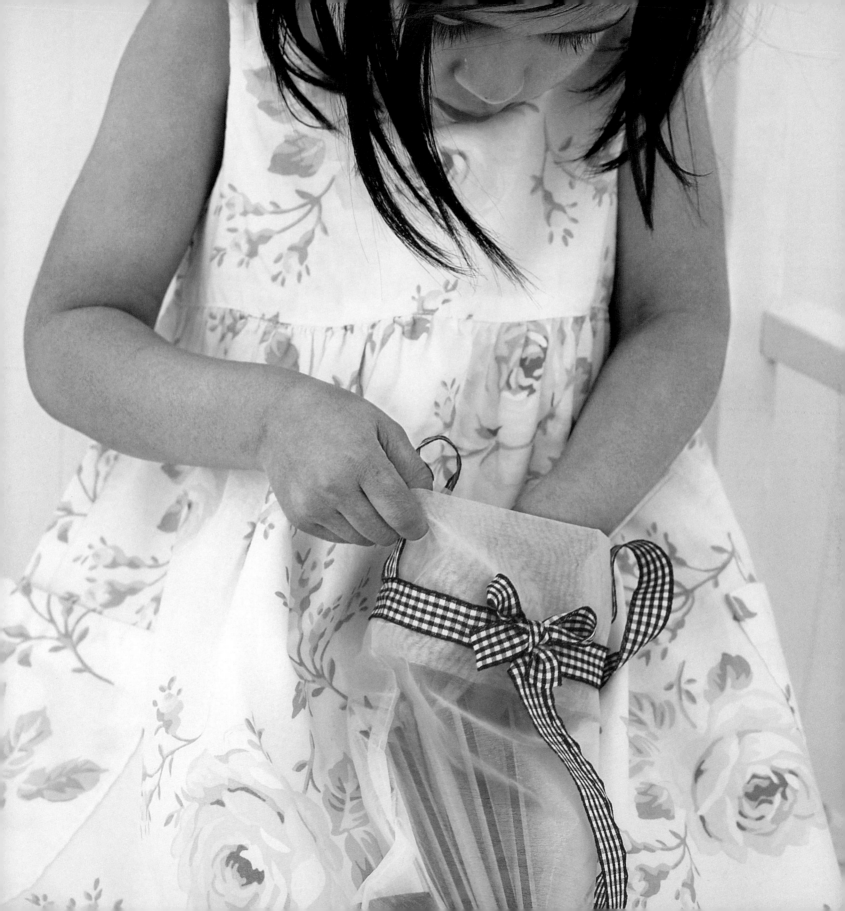

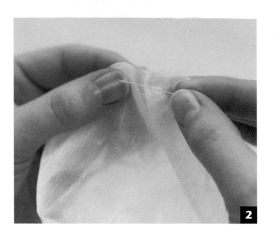

1 Cut the organza in half to give two strips measuring 65 x 15 cm (26 x 6 in). Taking one strip, fold one short end of the fabric down by 7.5 cm (3 in). Pin and machine-stitch a straight line across this end, 4 cm (1½ in) down from the fold. Leave a 12 mm (½ in) gap, then pin and machine-stitch a second line parallel to the first. Repeat at the opposite end of the fabric strip.

2 Fold the fabric in half, so that the two short ends come together. Make sure that the stitched folds face out. Pin and machine-stitch the sides, taking a 6 mm (¼ in) seam. To square off the bottom of the bag, pull each long edge down by 2.5 cm (1 in), flatten, and machine-stitch along the crease. Turn the bag right side out.

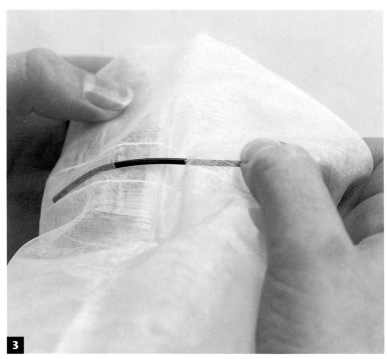

3 Cut the wire to a length of 25 cm (10 in) and snip a small hole at each end of the stitched parallel lines, just big enough to feed the wire through the top section of the bag. Secure the wire in place with a few hand stitches.

4 Cut 25 cm (10 in) of the ribbon and make a handle for the bag by gluing each end of the ribbon to one side of the bag – from the top of the bag down to the wired section. Glue another 25 cm (10 in) length of ribbon all around the bag, to conceal the wired section, bringing the ends to meet in the middle at the front of the bag.

• Before making the bags, think about how they may be used and adjust the sizes accordingly.

• Remember that gauzy fabrics like organza allow you to see what is in the bag, so choose the contents very carefully.

5 Use a third, 20 cm (8 in), length of ribbon to make a tied bow. Glue this to the front of the bag, where the two ends of the second strip of ribbon meet. Place the red card rectangle at the bottom of the bag to keep it square. Repeat all of the steps to make a second bag.

★ **Try this**

Try making a number of bags using the colours of the rainbow to work with a rainbow-themed room.

Use remnants of curtain and cushion fabrics from any themed bedroom to complete the look.

See also...

• Jewellery Tree, on page 104.

• Beautiful Bed Canopy, on page 128.

rocket lamp

This original rocket lamp can be made in less than a day and is a fitting addition to a room with a cosmic theme. Once you have the basic shape, your child can have fun designing the decoration for the fabric shade – windows, doors, lights and even an alien or two!

easy

4 hours

boys

suitable for a
helping hand

you will need

- Two 40 x 30 cm (16 x 12 in) sheets card for templates (see Templates, page 132)
- 80 x 25 cm x 18 mm (32 x 10 x ¾ in) MDF panel
- Pencil
- Eraser
- Jigsaw
- Dust mask
- Sanding block
- Fine-grade sandpaper
- 125 ml (4 fl oz) wood primer
- 2.5 cm (1 in) paintbrush
- Tape measure
- Acrylic paint:
  small tube red
  small tube blue
  small tube green
- 6 mm (¼ in) artist's paintbrush

- Masking tape
- 7.5 x 2.5 cm (3 x 1 in) self-adhesive hook-and-loop fastener
- Scissors
- 20 cm (8 in) fluorescent tube light (battery-operated)
- 137.5 cm (55 in) medium-weight coated wire
- Wire cutters
- 55 x 28.5 cm (21 x 11½ in) white cotton fabric
- 100 cm x 12 mm (40 x ½ in) bonding web
- Iron and board
- Glue gun
- Staple gun
- Picture hook and screws
- Screwdriver

2

3

1 Make a card template of the rocket on page 138. Place it on the MDF panel and draw around it in pencil. Cut out the shape using a jigsaw and sand all edges until smooth.

2 Prime the MDF panel and leave to dry. Once dry, paint the bottom 10 cm (4 in) of the panel red, with the 2.5 cm (1 in) paintbrush, and the top 15 cm (6 in) of the panel blue. Mask off each section to ensure a crisp line.

3 Cut the self-adhesive hook-and-loop fastener into three pieces and stick one half of each to the fluorescent-tube light fitting – top, middle and bottom. Stick the second half to corresponding positions (vertically) in the centre of the rocket panel and attach the light fitting.

4 Now make the rocket light shade. Mask off two 2.5 cm (1 in) stripes down the right-hand side and a panel to the left on the piece of white fabric. Paint using red, blue and green acrylic paints. Leave to dry.

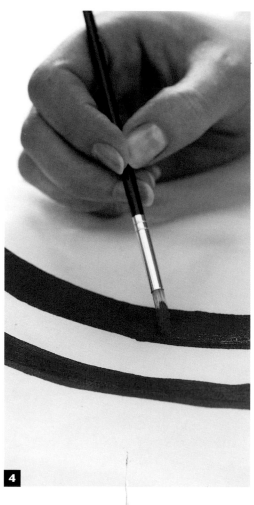

4

5

5 Measure and cut the coated wire into five equal lengths of 27.5 cm (11 in). Lay the white fabric out (portrait) on a flat surface and position one length of wire, horizontally, 12 mm (½ in) down from the top edge. Lay a 27.5 cm (11 in) strip of webbing directly beneath the wire and fold the top edge of the white fabric over. Iron in place, and repeat the process at the bottom edge of the fabric.

6 Position the remaining three lengths of wire at equal distances between the top and bottom wires (every 12.5 cm/5 in) and secure in place using a small amount of glue at each end and in the middle. Fold the two long, raw edges of the fabric over and secure with bonding web, sealing all ends of the wire.

7 Attach the fabric shade to the MDF rocket by holding both upright and stapling the fabric to the back of rocket, bending the wires to fit the MDF shape. The top of the shade should align with the bottom of the blue-painted section. Finally, fix a picture hook to the back of the rocket for hanging.

 Top tips

• Using a battery-powered light ensures that you have no trailing wires.

• Always be sure to use a low-voltage bulb.

★ Try this

Create a sky-at-night frieze. Attach a picture hook to the back of the light and mount on a midnight blue wall, jetting off into a moonlit, star- and planet-filled sky.

See also...

• Rocket Pyjama Case, on page 64.

• Star and Moon Blind, on page 124.

quick fixes and
finishing touches

jewellery tree

Your daughter will enjoy helping you make this vibrant jewellery tree and will love using it to display her prized collection of sparkly accessories. You can adjust the height of the tree or add more branches depending on how much jewellery there is!

easy

2 hours

girls

suitable for a helping hand

you will need

- 175 cm (70 in) medium-weight coated wire
- Tape measure
- Wire cutters
- 500 cm x 12 mm (200 x ½ in) red ribbon
- Glue gun
- Scissors
- 7.5 x 7.5 cm (3 x 3 in) red flowerpot (7.5 cm/3 in diameter at top)
- 7.5 x 5 cm (3 x 2 in) oasis block
- Craft knife
- Pencil
- 20 cm (8 in) square red card
- 15 x 15 cm (6 x 6 in) white organza
- 35 cm x 18 mm (14 x ¾ in) red gingham ribbon

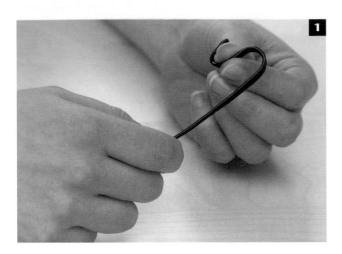

1 Measure and cut the wire to the following lengths: one at 25 cm (10 in); two at 35 cm (14 in); and two at 40 cm (16 in). Fold each in half, then bend and shape the top to look like a hook.

2 Take each length in turn and, starting at the top, begin to wind the red ribbon around the wire stem, making sure you completely cover the end of the wire first, and overlapping half the width of the ribbon as you go. Secure the ribbon in place by gluing at 2.5 cm (1 in) intervals. On reaching the bottom of the stem, cut off any extra ribbon and glue to secure the end.

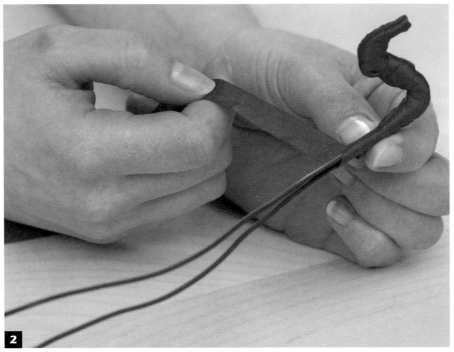

3 Once all five ribbon stems are complete, bunch them together and wrap ribbon 2.5 cm (1 in) deep around the bottom of all stems and glue to secure.

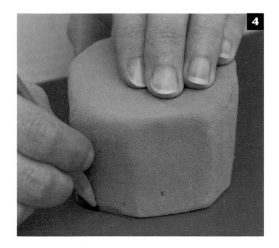

4 Use a craft knife to shape the oasis so that it fits inside the base of the flowerpot and make a small hole in the centre using a pencil – just large enough to fit the base of the bound wire stems. Trace the outline of the oasis on the red card and cut out so that the card fits neatly over the top. Make a hole in the centre of the card using a craft knife.

5 Loosely wrap the white organza around the oasis and card and, with glue around the ribbon section, push the bound wire stems and organza through the hole in the oasis until it reaches the bottom. Spread glue around the bottom and sides of the pot (inside) and place the organza-wrapped base and stems into position.

6 Bend and position each stem to achieve the desired tree effect. Finally, glue a little of the red gingham ribbon around the pot, approximately 12 mm (½ in) down from the top edge.

 Top tip

• Think about the types of jewellery you need to display – rings, necklaces, bracelets, for example – before making the tree, and adjust the heights of the branches to suit.

★ **Try this**

For a more rustic look, try using a terracotta pot and copper wire, omitting the ribbon altogether.

See also...

• Pretty Voile Pockets, on page 94.

• Beautiful Bed Canopy, on page 128.

tiger tie-backs

The perfect finishing touch for a room with a jungle theme (see also pages 74 and 90), these curtain ties are easy to make and can be a fun project for you to involve your child in. You could easily adapt the project to make furry cats for a toddler.

 easy

 4 hours

 girls and boys

 suitable for a helping hand

you will need

- 30 x 20 cm (12 x 8 in) paper for templates (see Templates, page 132)
- Scissors
- Felt:
  60 x 30 cm (24 x 12 in) orange
  15 x 15 cm (6 x 6 in) brown
  10 x 10 cm (4 x 4 in) yellow
  5 x 2.5 cm (2 x 1 in) beige
- Sewing pins
- Black felt-tip pen
- 30 x 15 cm x 12 mm (12 x 6 x ½ in) wadding
- Fabric glue (optional)
- Needle
- Orange sewing thread
- Brown embroidery thread
- 90 cm (36 in) thick cord

1 Make paper templates of the tiger and all details on page 139.

2 Fold the orange felt into four layers and pin the tiger template on top. Cut through all layers of felt to make four tiger shapes. Fold the wadding in half and repeat the process so that you have two wadding tiger shapes. Use the remaining templates to cut the brown felt stripes, the yellow felt face and inner ears, and the beige felt nose. Fold each colour felt in half to produce two of everything.

3 Use the template as a guide to attach the felt details to two of the orange tiger pieces, using fabric glue or stitching in orange thread.

4 Make sure that the tigers face in opposite directions. Use brown embroidery thread to sew the eye and mouth details.

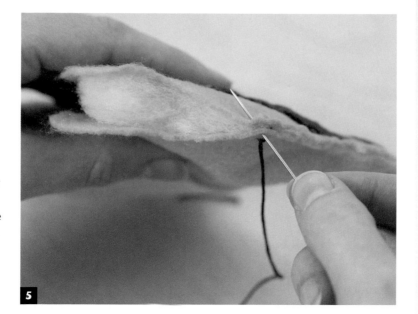

Top tip

• In order to make two identical tigers facing in opposite directions, you may find it easier to trace the template using tracing paper, which can then be flipped to produce a mirror image.

5 Sandwich the wadding between a plain tiger shape and a detailed tiger shape. Using brown embroidery thread, hand-stitch the outline of the tiger, about 6 mm (¼ in) in from the edge of the felt and round his head (see the template), using a running stitch through all three layers. Repeat for the second tiger.

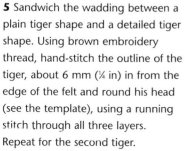

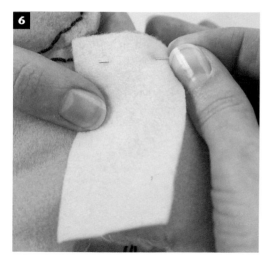

6 Use orange thread to oversew the edges of each tiger, fully enclosing the wadding. Finally, take two off-cuts of yellow or orange felt and attach to the back of each tiger to make a loop. Thread 45 cm (18 in) of thick cord through each loop and use to tie around each curtain.

★ Try this

Continue with the rainforest theme by making two colourful felt snakes, each long enough to wrap around a curtain, and tie.

See also...

• Rainforest Storage, on page 74.
• Sunflower Nightlight, on page 90.

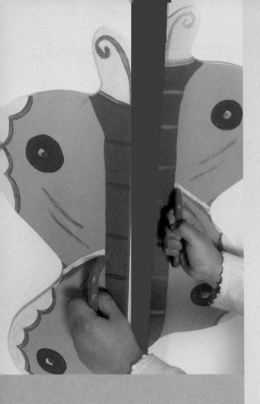

butterfly handles

This colourful pair of butterfly handles adds decorative detail to a wardrobe and makes the perfect finishing touch for a pink floral scheme (see also pages 10 and 52). You can draw the butterfly freehand, so have fun adapting the design with your child.

 easy

 4 hours

 girls

 suitable for a helping hand

you will need

- 40 x 30 cm (16 x 12 in) paper for template (see Templates, page 132)
- Scissors
- 40 x 30 cm x 15 mm (16 x 12 x ⅝ in) MDF panel
- Pencil
- Jigsaw
- Dust mask
- Sanding block
- Fine-grade sandpaper
- Matt emulsion paint:
  125 ml (4 fl oz) white
  125 ml (4 fl oz) beige
  125 ml (4 fl oz) fuchsia pink
  125 ml (4 fl oz) orange
- Small tube gold artist's paint
- 2.5 cm (1 in) paintbrush
- Fine artist's paintbrush
- 7.5 cm (3 in) plastic D handles with screws
- 125 ml (4 fl oz) clear varnish spray
- Tape measure
- Drill
- 6 mm (¼ in) drill bit
- Screwdriver

1 Make a paper template of half the butterfly using the shape on page 140. Align the straight edge of the template with one long edge of the MDF and draw round it in pencil. Flip the template over and repeat on the second long edge of MDF. Cut around both shapes using a jigsaw and lightly sand all edges smooth.

2 Prime all surfaces of the MDF using white emulsion and a 2.5 cm (1 in) paintbrush and, when dry, paint again using beige emulsion. When dry, refer to the template to draw the details on each wing. Then paint, using fuchsia pink for the body, orange for the spots and white for the wing tips.

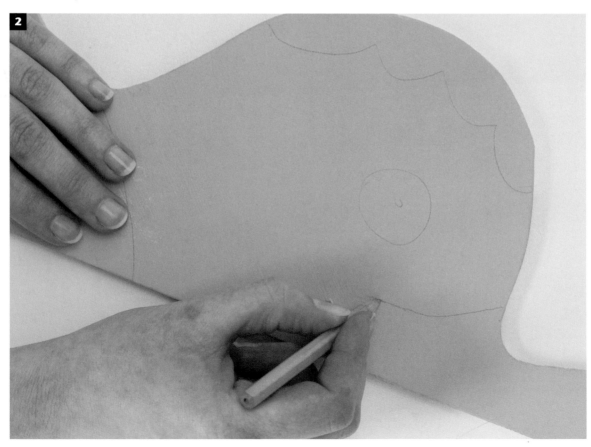

3 Use the gold paint and artist's brush for outlines and finer details on the body, wings, antennae and spots. While the butterfly is drying, paint the plastic door handles to match the butterfly body. Spray both wings with a coat of clear varnish and leave to dry.

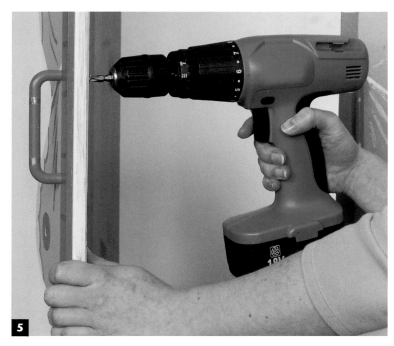

4 Measure and mark in pencil the position for each handle, at the centre of each butterfly wing and 2.5 cm (1 in) in from the straight edge. Drill a hole at an equal distance above and below the centre mark for the screws.

5 Align one butterfly wing on the wardrobe door and screw the handle through the wing and into the door. Repeat with the second butterfly wing.

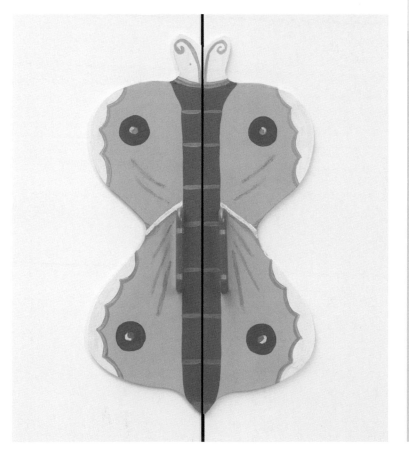

Top tip

• If making a design that does not have a template, draw half of the shape freehand on the MDF, then cut out using a jigsaw. Flip the cut shape to make a second, identical piece.

★ Try this

For a room with a football theme, draw around a large plate onto the MDF. Cut out and then cut in half. Paint on a football design and secure in the same way.

See also...

• Drop-leaf Flower Desk, on page 10.
• Pretty Pocket Bed Throw, on page 52.

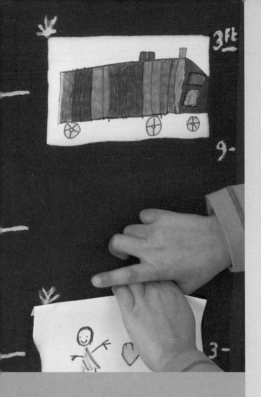

picture height chart

This innovative design for a height chart encourages you and your child to keep a visual record of her growth as she gets older. Simply take a photo or ask your child to draw a picture when you measure her each year and slip it into the pocket next to her height mark.

 easy

 3 hours

 girls and boys

 suitable for a helping hand

you will need

- 120 x 50 cm (48 x 20 in) red felt
- Tape measure
- Scissors
- 7.5 x 12.5 cm (3 x 5 in) card template
- Fine black felt-tip pen
- Sewing machine
- Red sewing thread
- 3D fabric paint:
  50 ml (2 fl oz) yellow
  50 ml (2 fl oz) black
- 300 cm x 12 mm (120 x ½ in) red
  velvet ribbon
- Glue gun
- Two screw hooks

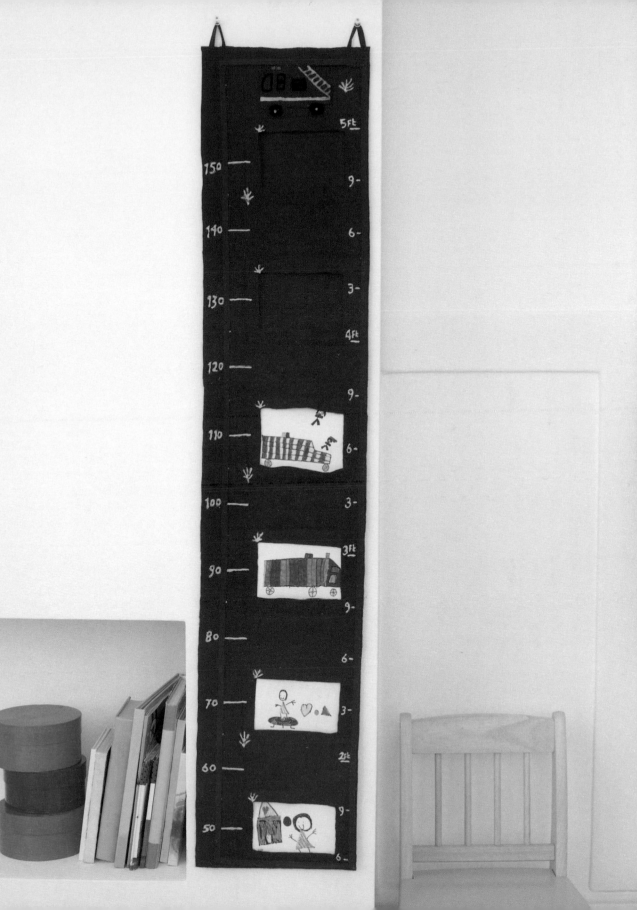

1 Measure and cut the felt in half widthways to give you two 120 x 25 cm (48 x 10 in) panels.

2 Using the card template, mark six landscape rectangles in one of the panels. Start at the bottom, placing the template 12 mm (½ in) up and 5 cm (2 in) from the left of the panel. Draw around the template lightly, using the black felt-tip pen.

3 Position the template 10 cm (4 in) above the first drawn rectangle and mark in the same way. Repeat, moving up the felt panel, until you have drawn six rectangles. Cut each one out using scissors, and set one cut rectangle aside.

4 Machine-stitch the two panels together, sewing 2.5 cm (1 in) in from the left-hand edge, and 12 mm (½ in) in from the top, bottom and right-hand edges. Now sew a 12 mm (½ in) frame around the six cut-out rectangles.

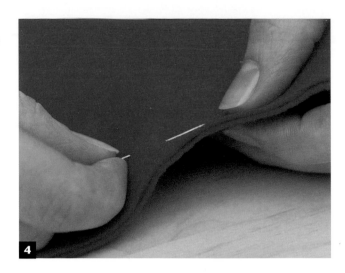

5 Use a tape measure and the black felt-tip pen to mark metric and imperial heights respectively on the left- and right-hand edges of the height chart. For the metric measurements, start 6 cm from the bottom. The first of the metric marks should read 50 cm and should rise in 10 cm increments to 150 cm. For the imperial measurements, start ⅞ in from the bottom of the chart. The first of the imperial marks should read 6 in and should rise in 6 in increments to 5 ft.

6 Write each measurement in black felt-tip pen and draw a 5 cm (2 in) long indicator line. Paint over the numbers and lines using the yellow fabric paint and leave to dry.

7 With the rectangle set aside in step 3, cut out the fire engine using the shape on page 139. Paint the detail using the yellow and black fabric paint. When dry, glue the motif in place at the top of the height chart 2.5 cm (1 in) down from the top. Paint a few flames on the chart.

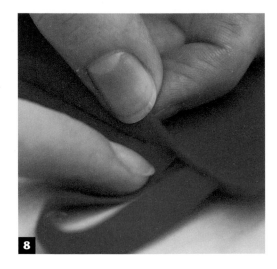

8 Cut four lengths of red velvet ribbon: two 100 cm (40 in) long and two 20 cm (8 in) long and use to cover the stitched frame of the height chart. Attach using the glue gun. Use the same ribbon to make 5 cm (2 in) loops for the top of the chart, gluing each 2.5 cm (1 in) in from the left and right and placing them between the front and back panels.

9 Hang the height chart on the wall, using two screw hooks from which to hang the loops. Pay special attention to the position of the chart on the wall: the bottom of the chart needs to be 45 cm (17¾ in) from the floor in order for the heights to be accurate when measured.

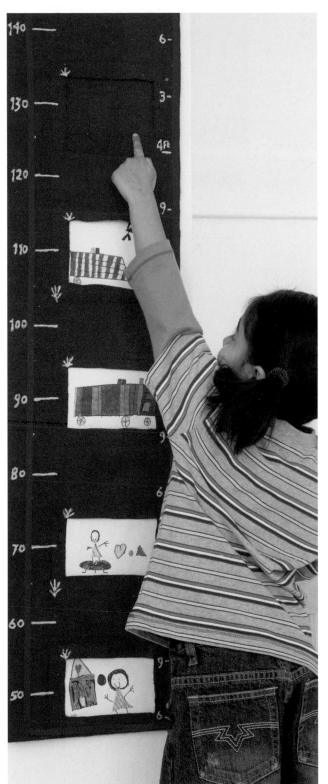

 Top tips

• To keep the tape measure in place as you mark the height measurements, it may help to use a little blue tack.

• Be sparing with any extra details, as the pictures and photos will add colour and interest, too.

★ Try this

Make a flower height chart. Instead of painting the numbers directly onto the felt, cut out small flowers from different colours of felt (approximately 2.5 cm/1 in diameter), and paint the height markings onto these before positioning on the height chart.

See also...

• Fire-engine Bed, on page 40.

nursery
wall frieze

This sunny wall frieze makes the perfect accompaniment to the Bird Cot Mobile on page 60. It uses similar motifs, is inexpensive and can be assembled in no time. You can decide how many clouds and birds you make up. Encourage older siblings to help you choose.

you will need

- Three 40 x 30 cm (16 x 12 in) sheets of card for templates (see Templates, page 132)
- Scissors
- Foam sheets:
  40 x 30 cm (16 x 12 in) white
  40 x 30 cm (16 x 12 in) pastel yellow
  40 x 30 cm (16 x 12 in) yellow
- Fine ballpoint pen
- PVA glue
- Four 5 mm (⅛ in) diameter black self-adhesive spots
- Twelve 2.5 cm (1 in) double-sided adhesive foam pads
- Approximately 150 x 54 cm (59 x 21 in) blue wallpaper
- Wallpaper paste

easy

2 hours

girls and boys

suitable for a helping hand

1 Start by making card templates of the shapes on page 141.

2 Place the cloud template on the white foam sheet and draw around the shape using the ballpoint pen. Repeat at least twice more before cutting out the clouds using scissors.

3 Draw around the bird shapes in the same way, to make three bodies and one wing from the white foam sheet and one body, three wings and four beaks from the pastel yellow foam sheet. Cut out.

4 Glue a yellow wing to a white bird and vice versa. Glue each beak to the underside of the bird's body. Stick a black spot on each bird for an eye.

5 To make the sun, use pastel yellow foam for the circle and yellow for the six triangular rays. Glue along one edge of each triangle and stick to the underside of the sun circle.

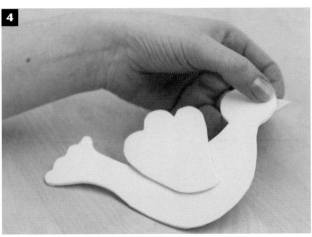

6 Paste the blue wallpaper onto the desired wall. Stick the self-adhesive foam pads to the backs of all foam pieces (two on each of the clouds and the sun, and one on each of the birds) and arrange your frieze.

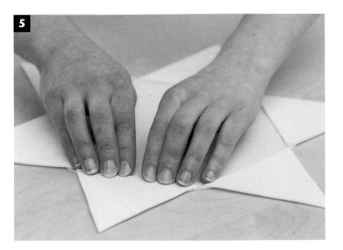

 Top tips

• Flip the template over to make birds flying in the opposite direction.

• To vary the sizes of the clouds, birds or sun, simply increase or decrease the template on a photocopier.

★ **Try this**

Make a three-dimensional frieze, using a touch light as the centre of the sun and foam triangles for the rays. Attach the birds and clouds to the wall using small coiled springs (at least 12 mm/½ in long) so that they stand out from the wall slightly.

See also...

• Bird Cot Mobile, on page 60.

• Pocket Cot Tidy, on page 70.

star and moon blind

Make a plain blind more exciting by jazzing it up with this silver star-and-moon design. By cutting out one or two of the stars you can allow some light through during the summer months while keeping the room dark enough for your child to sleep in.

you will need

- **25 x 25 x 2.5 cm (10 x 10 x 1 in) sponge (see Templates, page 132)**
- **Black felt-tip pen**
- **Scissors**
- **120 cm (48 in) midnight blue roller blind**
- **Pencil**
- **Ruler**
- **125 ml (4 fl oz) metallic silver paint**
- **Small plate**
- **Kitchen paper**
- **Craft knife**

easy

3 hours

boys

suitable for a helping hand

1 Start by making sponge templates of the shapes on page 140.

2 Lay the roller blind on a flat surface and measure and mark a faint horizontal pencil line, 7.5 cm (3 in) up from the bottom.

3 Pour some silver paint onto the plate and dip the 7.5 cm (3 in) star-shaped sponge into the paint. Dab the sponge on kitchen paper to remove excess paint, then sponge the first star 12.5 cm (5 in) in from the left-hand side of the blind, just above the pencil line. Continue to sponge stars across the blind, at 7.5 cm (3 in) intervals.

4 Use the 5 cm (2 in) sponge to paint a second row of stars, 10 cm (4 in) above the first row and leaving a 7.5 cm (3 in) gap in between each one. Start 40 cm (16 in) in from the left.

5 Paint three stars using the 2.5 cm (1 in) sponge, 10 cm (4 in) above the row below, but starting 65 cm (26 in) in from the left, at 3.75 cm (1½ in) intervals. Using the photograph on page 125 as a guide, sponge two small stars, 2.5 cm (1 in) centred above the last row and one small star centred above that.

6 To sponge in the moon shape, measure 20 cm (8 in) in from the right-hand side of the blind and 2.5 cm (1 in) above the last small star.

7 Once the paint is completely dry, use the craft knife to cut out some of the painted stars, leaving a 5 mm (⅛ in) silver frame for detail.

 Top tips

• If the blind is to be used primarily as a blackout blind, cut out fewer, or no, stars.

• Check the height of your window to make sure the design can be seen fully when the blind is drawn. If not, adjust to fit.

★ Try this

To give the blind an even more cosmic theme, sponge on some small planets and even a small rocket heading for the moon.

See also...

• Rocket Pyjama Case, on page 64.

• Rocket Lamp, on page 98.

beautiful
bed canopy

Quick to assemble, this light, flowing canopy adds an air of mystique to a girl's bedroom. The decoration is simple – a number of red and white bows, which your child can help you to attach – but the effect is striking.

 easy

 2 hours

 girls

 suitable for a helping hand

you will need

- 340 x 2.5 cm (134 x 1 in) red gingham ribbon
- Tape measure
- Scissors
- Needle
- White sewing thread
- White mosquito net

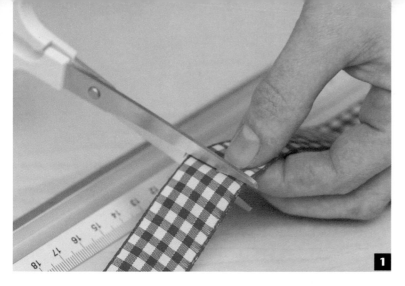

1 Cut ten 10 cm (4 in) lengths and ten 17.5 cm (7 in) lengths of the ribbon and tie each one into a bow.

 Top tip

• You can adapt the design of the net to work in any number of themed rooms, using remnants of your curtain or bed linen fabrics.

2 Hand stitch each ribbon through the centre of the bow, so that it does not come loose.

3 Glue each bow to the mosquito net, in a random pattern, but alternating between the two lengths and keeping each one approximately 15 cm (6 in) apart.

4 Cut a 50 cm (20 in) length of ribbon and attach it to the top of the net. Tie the two loose ends together and hang the net according to the manufacturer's instructions.

★ Try this

Create a dazzling garden theme by cutting out three or four white fabric clouds, a yellow fabric sun, several yellow, orange and pink fabric flowers and a few strands of green fabric grass. Glue the grass around the bottom of the net, the flowers above the grass and the sun and clouds towards the top.

See also...

• Pretty Voile Pockets, on page 94.
• Jewellery Tree, on page 104.

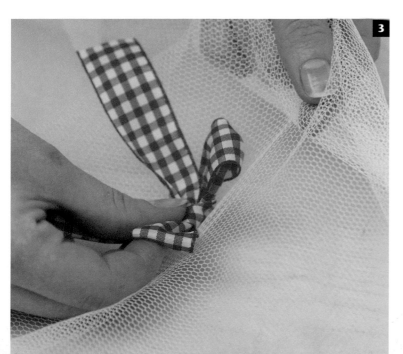

beautiful bed canopy **131**

templates

The following templates and stencils are used in several projects in this book, where instructions are given. Some templates can be copied same-size (100%), others may require enlarging on a photocopier, see the percentage given with each template. Some are also used as guides for decoration or embellishment. You can, of course, use the templates at any size you like or, indeed, for different projects altogether.

Making and using paper and card templates

Photocopy the template onto paper or thin card (make sure the card is thin enough to fit in the machine), enlarging or reducing the size as required. Cut the shape out using sharp scissors. You can use the template to cut fabric and sponge shapes by pinning the template to the fabric or sponge and cutting out, or by drawing around the template, removing it, then cutting out. For drawing onto wood, you may want to attach a little (low-tack) double-sided adhesive tape or folded masking tape to the back of the template to keep it secure.

Making and using acetate stencils

Photocopy the template onto paper, enlarging or reducing the size as required. Place the acetate over the photocopy and trace the design using a felt-tip pen. (If you have access to a photocopier, and the size of acetate fits, you can photocopy the image straight onto the acetate.) Use a craft knife and cutting mat to cut out the stencil. For the best results, secure the template to a project using masking tape, and have kitchen paper to hand for removing excess paint from the sponge or brush as you go.

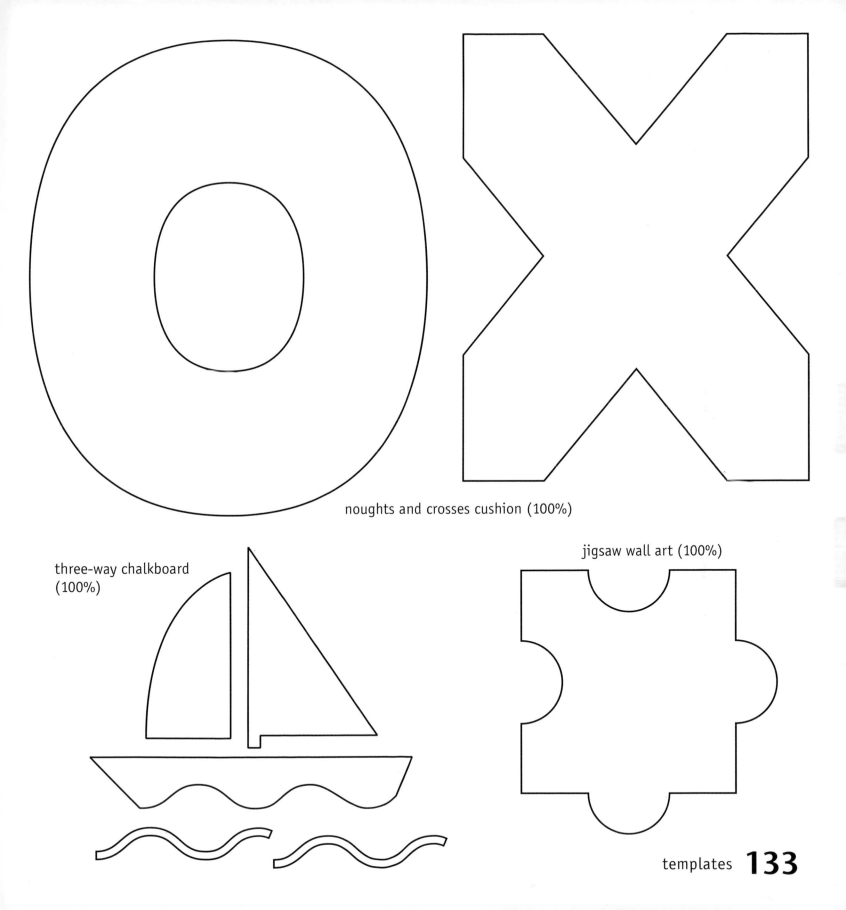

noughts and crosses cushion (100%)

three-way chalkboard (100%)

jigsaw wall art (100%)

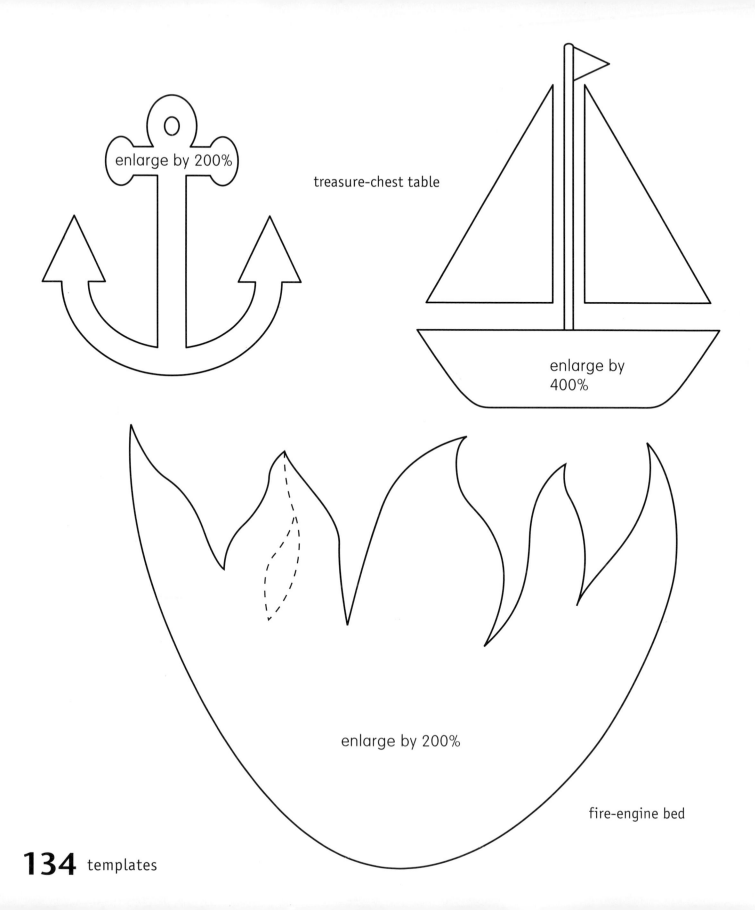

enlarge by 200%

treasure-chest table

enlarge by
400%

enlarge by 200%

fire-engine bed

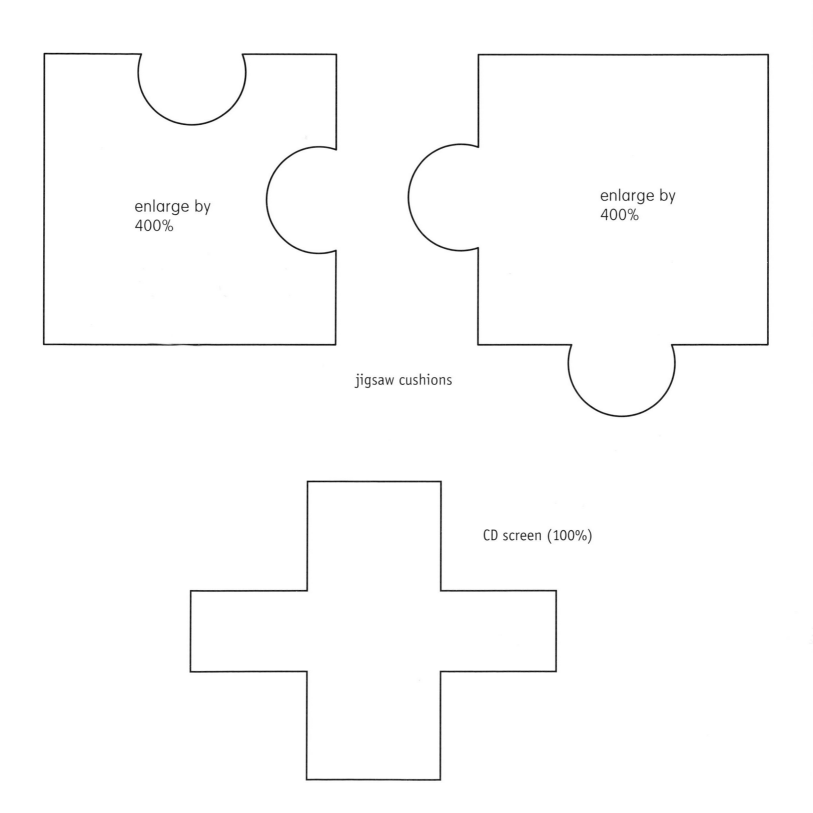

enlarge by 400%

enlarge by 400%

jigsaw cushions

CD screen (100%)

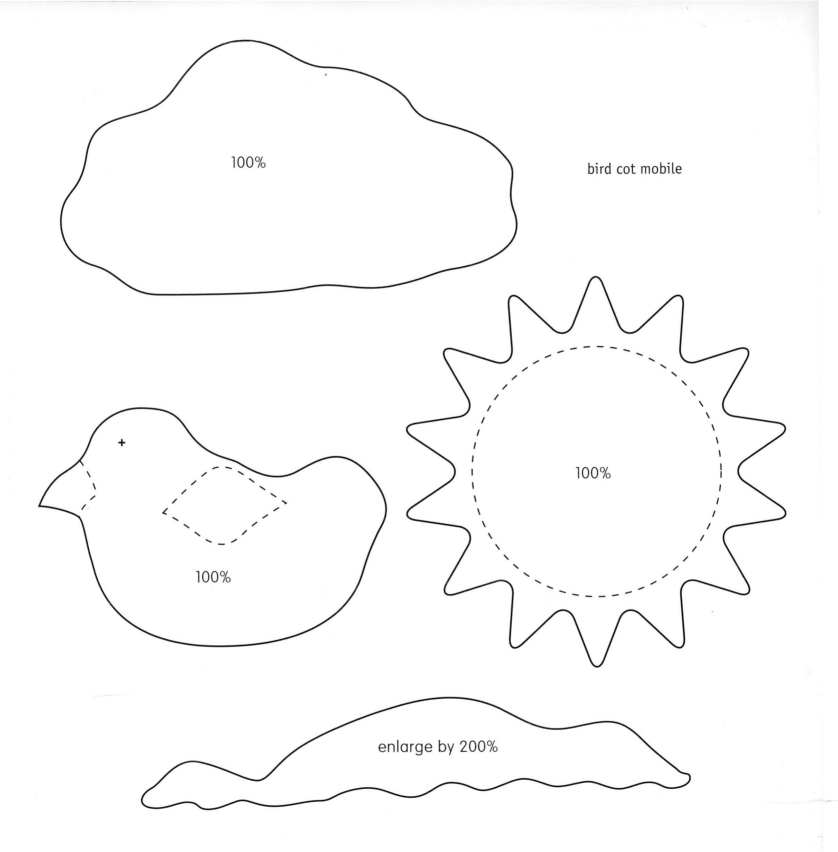

100%

bird cot mobile

100%

100%

100%

enlarge by 200%

rocket pyjama case (100%)

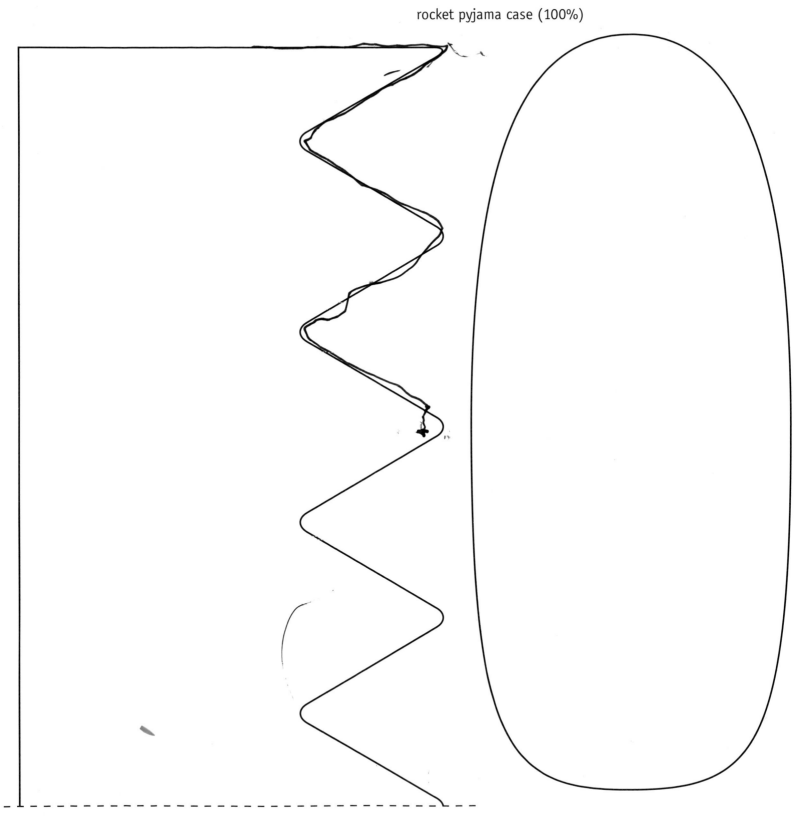

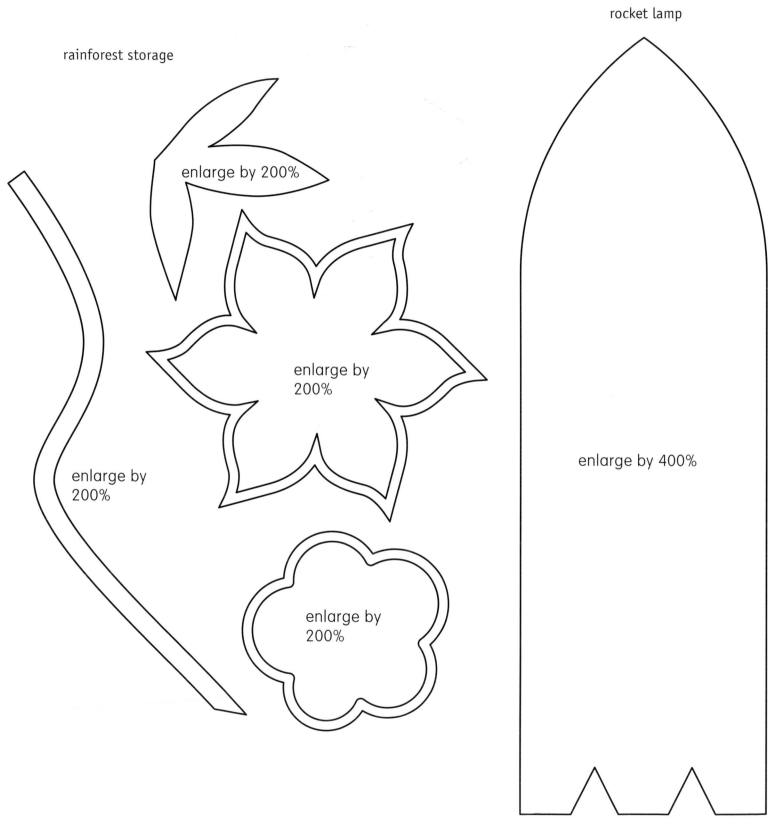

rainforest storage

enlarge by 200%

enlarge by 200%

enlarge by
200%

enlarge by
200%

enlarge by
200%

rocket lamp

enlarge by 400%

picture height chart (100%)

tiger tie-backs (100%)

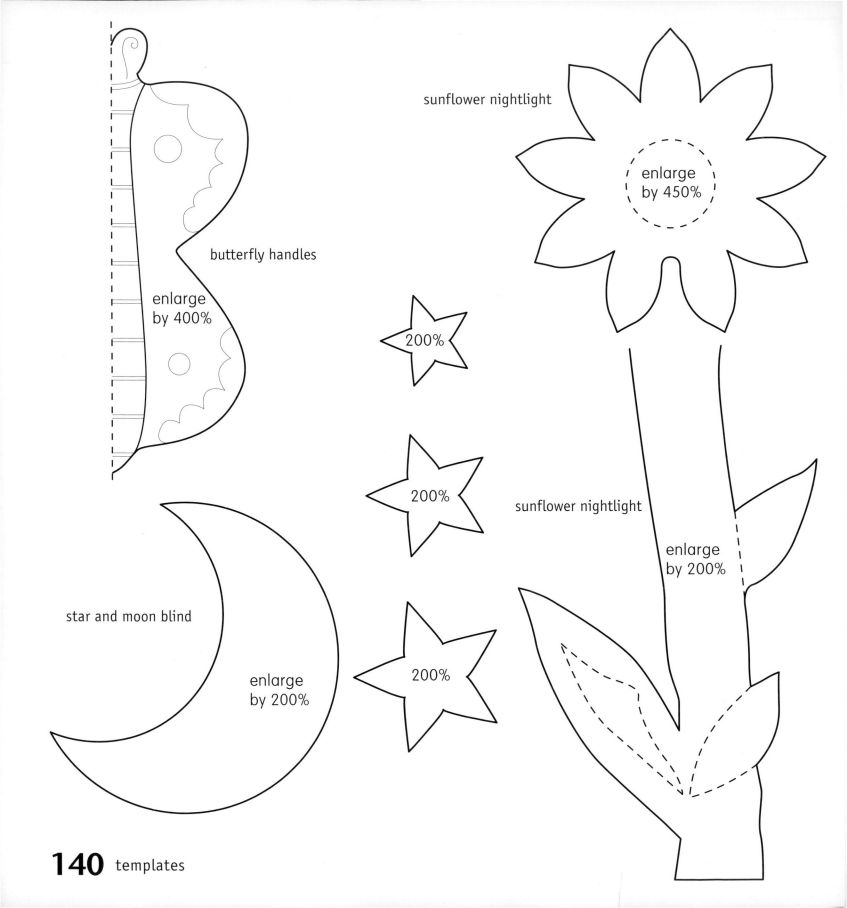

butterfly handles

enlarge
by 400%

sunflower nightlight

enlarge
by 450%

200%

200%

star and moon blind

enlarge
by 200%

200%

sunflower nightlight

enlarge
by 200%

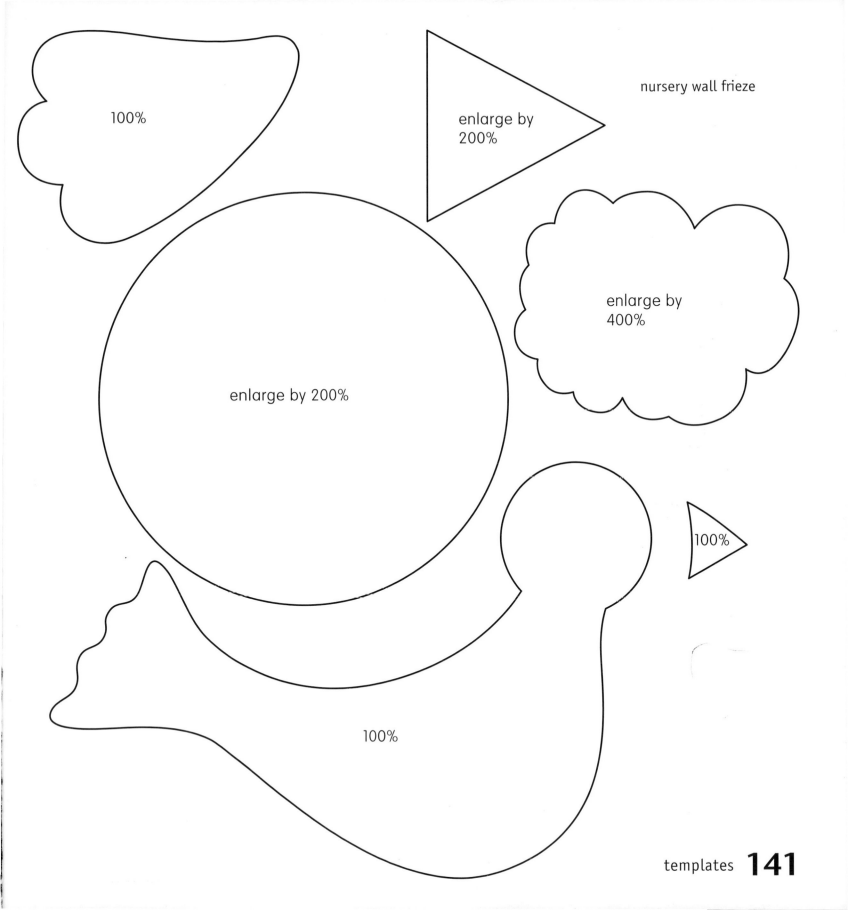

100%

enlarge by
200%

enlarge by
400%

enlarge by 200%

100%

100%

index

acknowledgements

I would like to thank the following people for their contributions to this book: Seamstress, Chrystalleni Lambrias; Soft Furnishings' Expert, Mary Knight; Crafts' Expert, Shoshana Abigail Gilmore; and Interior Designer, Deborah Lawson.

Thanks, also, to the carpentry department at Southgate College, North London - in particular to Gary Callard and Lee Usher.

Finally, thanks to my husband Chris Lambrias for his help with many of the projects and the writing; to my two beautiful girls Kiara and Michaela for inspiration; and to Mandy Schreiber, Pratima Myanger, Darren Burgess, Linda Blake and Stacey Robson for their support.

Executive Editor Katy Denny
Editor Emma Pattison
Executive Art Editor Penny Stock
Designer one2six
Photographer Adrian Pope
Illustrator Sudden Impact Media
Senior Production Controller Manjit Sihra